UNMARKED TRAILS

A Memoir

by

Jane Flink

Bloomington, IN Milton Keynes, UK

AuthorHouse™
1663 Liberty Drive, Suite 200
Bloomington, IN 47403
www.authorhouse.com
Phone: 1-800-839-8640

AuthorHouse™ UK Ltd.
500 Avebury Boulevard
Central Milton Keynes, MK9 2BE
www.authorhouse.co.uk
Phone: 08001974150

© 2007 Jane Flink. All rights reserved.

No part of this book may be reproduced, stored in a retrieval system, or transmitted by any means without the written permission of the author.

First published by AuthorHouse 6/19/2007

ISBN: 978-1-4343-0314-1 (e)
ISBN: 978-1-4343-0313-4 (sc)

Library of Congress Control Number: 2007902375

Printed in the United States of America
Bloomington, Indiana

This book is printed on acid-free paper.

Commentary

Jane Flink can write. Whether she's conjuring up an old buggy in the woods or pondering the passage of time, she finds the universal in the particular, the lasting in the fleeting. This is lovely stuff, lyrical and wise.

Bob Levin, Assistant National Editor
The Globe and Mail, Toronto

In this book, Jane Flink reflects on years of living. As she writes, "Life goes on. It sounds like an easy out, a callous maxim, an unfeeling dismissal. In reality, it is one of the most comforting elements of our world." She makes us long for the comfort of her "Treasure in the Woods," where the land surrounding her home in northern Boone County reflected nature. These and dozens of other situations, incidents and issues will return you, the reader, to your past. Relax and reflect. This journey is as refreshing in retrospect as it was when initially experienced.

Dr. William H. Taft
Professor Emeritus, University of Missouri School of Journalism
2004 Missouri Honor Medalist for
Distinguished Service in Journalism

After 25 years of friendship with Jane Flink, I remain ever eager to *absorb* her stories and perspectives, which are too fine, too rich to simply consume. Slow down and soak up these pleasurable reflections. Indeed, you might even be able to improve upon the experience…read them out loud to another story-lover.

Vicki Russell, Associate Publisher
Columbia Daily Tribune

Jane Flink writes from many perspectives: editor, business owner, community economic developer, reporter, historian, humorist, wife, mother, grandmother, daughter of the South, housekeeper, nature lover, and more. Her writing is unique, reflecting her many interests and wealth of knowledge. You can always be sure when reading Jane's work that it is straight from the heart, written with a precision and crispness few others can match.

Bruce Wallace, Editor and Publisher
Boone County Journal

Dedication

For my husband, Richard A. Flink.
Whenever a project seems overwhelming, he says,
"Of course you can do it,"
and that has made all the difference.

Acknowledgments

I am indebted to Dr. Bill Taft who, from the beginning of this project, shared his vested knowledge and experience to help me get it right. Heartfelt thanks to Jo Sapp, whose vision enhances her skill as an editor, and to Barbara Rothschild, a discerning reader and critic.

Dr. Kit Salter's firm and expert intervention deserves my lasting gratitude, as does Gay Bumgarner's gift of her creative genius. Several close friends and family members have read, suggested, commented and contributed. All of them played a role in shaping the product this book has become.

Introduction

On a spring morning in 2001 I sat at my desk in the newsroom working on my final edition of the *Boone County Journal,* turning over the last page of the news section of the paper, the page editors call "the second front." Next week a new owner would take charge. What is it like, I thought, to retire, to have nothing to do? Is there life after journalism?

My husband Dick and I bought the *Journal* in 1986 with hardly a second thought. I had more than a decade of journalism behind me; he had retired as a corporate executive. What we bought was a four-page local weekly, barely kept alive by part-time owners operating out of a closet in the back of a floral shop. We brought to this new acquisition drive, determination and an inflated vision of our abilities. "Desk-top publishing" was the rage in 1986, so we rented office space and installed Macintosh computers and an Apple printer. Our desks came from garage sales and Dick built slant boards for the composing room. We were set on giving our readers a real broadsheet newspaper.

Over the next 15 years new housing in the city of Ashland, Missouri sprang up like mushrooms after a spring rain. With the jump in population and commerce the newspaper grew and prospered. But by 2001 the aging owners had pretty much given up chasing fire engines. The decision to sell the newspaper was far more complex than our leap to buy it. We had a lot to learn when we casually purchased a newspaper, but that was nothing compared to the learning curve ahead as we entered the life cycle called retirement.

I woke up my first morning as a retired person with a clear calendar and a strange hollow feeling. I had developed no strategies for doing nothing, had never given a thought to acclimating myself to an unstructured life. I loved my profession with all my heart and my work consumed my every waking moment. It seemed likely that retirement would be a crash course in the pursuit of meaning.

I had always said I would never retire. It is easy for high-energy people to get hooked on excitement and hard to train them to the slower pace aging requires. Growing up, I was the third by eight years of three sisters in a family that expressed its high energy in verbal calisthenics. By far the youngest, my role was to listen where listening was a precious gift. In our household a heated debate could rise over dinner about the values and tragedies of the French Revolution, and the debate might continue at breakfast the next morning. Fragmentary thoughts and half-formed sentences floated on the breeze that blew billowing white curtains into airy rooms. The fragments were always there for someone to snatch down and reinsert in the endless rounds of talk. I learned the fine art of blending with my background, the better to hear and observe. And I was free at any time to reach up and capture choice fragments of my own to write about.

For better or worse I have been a writer all my life. I wrote my first book when I was nine years old and won a state teachers' blue ribbon for it. I was blessed with a child's uncluttered mind and the passion for language that infected my entire family

At 18, I took the train west from my New Jersey home to Carleton College in Northfield, Minnesota, boldly assuming kinship with the early settlers of my new world. I tested into Creative Writing 201, wrote for the campus newspaper, and sighed with relief over bluebooks with essay questions.

After college I lived in England and traveled in Europe. With the help of historian A. L. Rowse, I signed on at Oxford colleges to audit such oddly appealing classes as "The Importance of Hedgerows in English History" and "An Introduction to Middle English Literature." At age 23, home again in New York state, I met and married Dick Flink, a young corporate engineer specializing in time and motion study. We produced five children in six and a half years and moved frequently as his job transfers took us to a sampling of America's cities.

I was a stay-at-home mom until I was 40 when our nest began to empty out as children went off to college. To cushion the shock I took a reporter's job at a small newspaper in central Missouri. With a late start, I knew I had to move fast. In short order I progressed from weekly newspaper to daily newspaper to monthly magazine, to director of the Winston Churchill Memorial and Library at Westminster College in Fulton, Missouri and in 1986, at age 57, to newspaper co-owner, editor and publisher.

Fifteen years later I packed up the career I loved, and stored it in my memory banks. To age gracefully is to learn to cope with increasing disability, a wise woman once told me. To admit and accept that you are face to face with the grim reality of relentless time.

And so the day came when we handed over the keys to the office and stepped off into the deep end to explore a more contemplative life in our house on a lake in the fragrant woods of southern Boone County. Dick was 79 and ready for a second retirement. I was 72, probing the places where grief dwelt hand in hand with guilt, reluctant to leave my life as a writer, my daily contact with writers, teaching writers, editing writers, pulling all the writing together and sending it out to a community of loyal readers.

Writing still leads me to my clearest realities. My weekly newspaper columns document my newly unstructured life. Daily I learn to live in my house again, not just eat and sleep here; to set goals and hone skills. I have written a column a week for 20 years, so the drill is habitual. In my home office each Monday, as I turn musing into essay, I am comforted by the familiar tyranny of the weekly deadline.

The essays columnists write trickle forth from teasing streams of delicious words and unfinished thoughts like those that swirled through the airy rooms of my childhood. The best essays blend the ephemera of individual perception with the universality of human experience. Each essay in this book, written between 2003 and 2006, takes the form of the day it was born and doesn't bend easily to the discipline of chronology.

Week by week, I reflect on this transitive period in a life blessed by the grace of God with friends and family, variety and texture, adventure and achievement, tempered by occasional misconstruction and transfigured by a powerful sense of place. On and off these pages, I negotiate the terms of my journey, understanding that my passport contains outdated material and my visa has a limited duration. There is no closure in this life – when one door swings shut another opens and we walk through into a briarpatch of new experience.

Here, then, are the everyday observations of a former media person, scattered like breadcrumbs to guide others through their own tangles of unmarked trails. Is there life after journalism? In retirement as in all life passages, if we listen, absorb and observe, in time we come to treasure these new places, to own them, even to call them home.

- Jane Duncan Flink
Hartsburg, Missouri 2006

Contents

I. **THE SECOND FRONT**

   Life After Journalism 1

   Small Towns Leave The Light On For You 5

   When Canada Geese Made The News 9

   The Newsroom Chili Wars 12

   Once A Reporter... 15

   Old Songs Go Round and Round 18

   It's All About Light 20

   Creative Tools 23

II. **LEARNING FROM LIVING**

   The Deep End 27

   Shadow Selves At Your Service 30

   Always Lie About Your Age 32

   When Charlie Ravioli Came To Town 35

   Bringing The Harvest Home 38

   The Passages Of Time 41

   The Relevance Of Final Gifts 44

   Life Goes On 47

III. **BEGUILED BY PLACE**

   Treasure In The Woods 51

   The Shape Of Home 54

      The Ins And Outs Of Downsizing 56

      Color Me Glad 59

      Spring In Missouri 61

      A Monument To Broken Dreams 64

      Why We Live Here 66

      A Garage Of My Own 68

      Waiting For The Rain 71

      Lights Out 73

IV.   WANDERING WOMAN

      When I Am Old 77

      Country Roads Have Tales To Tell 80

      An Urgency Of Surrender 83

      Hear That Lonesome Whistle 85

      Vacation Preparation 88

      The Romance Of Motoring 90

      The Unfriendly Skies 93

      Hawaii, My Love 95

      Late Winter Journey 99

      Wilderness Beckons 101

V.   ROOTS AND TIES

      Parents Pass It On 105

      The Art Of Visiting 108

      When Guests Leave 111

      Long Autumn Thoughts 113

Through Revolving Doors 117
Friendships Can Last A Lifetime 119
An Independent Fourth Of July 122
The Elephant You Never Forget 124
The Survey Says… 127
Happily Ever After 130

Chapter One: The Second Front

LIFE AFTER JOURNALISM

When I go to town and run into old friends they ask me how I like retirement and if I miss being editor of the local newspaper. It isn't an easy question to answer. I backed into journalism in the mid 1970s and left it in 2001, lucky to the end. From start to finish, I loved my work.

When I began as a temp at the *Centralia Fireside Guard* in 1974 I had the usual illusions about small town newspapers and none of the benefits of a J-school background. Linotypes clunked in the back of the old building, telephones were black handsets and our mechanical typewriters had a prehistoric look. The first thing I wrote was a photo caption. It must have been a good enough caption because they kept me and when a new editor bought the paper and modernized the shop, I was part of the package. My friend Arlene did the society news and I wrote city council and cop shop pieces and chased fires, car wrecks and disasters.

I had disasters of my own. I took to paste-up like a mouse to cheese, so too soon the old hands left me alone one night in an empty building with an election tabloid to assemble. I lacked one crucial piece of information: Tabloid pages come two to a sheet and you number them

1 on the right-hand page and 8 on the left, 2 on the left and 7 on the right, and so on. I numbered mine in sequence and the printer sent back 5,000 copies of the worst mess you ever saw. Our advertisers had fits. My editor said it was a learning experience and docked my pay. After he stopped shouting.

The election over, I went scrounging for numbers that would show how our people voted. By midnight everybody had gone home and I was still getting busy signals at the county clerk's office. I knew one thing – the Associated Press gets first crack at news, so I called the Kansas City bureau. A nice man asked me if my wire was down. "Wire?" I asked. There was a pause. "What paper is this again?" he said. When I told him he laughed. "Hang on," he said and when he came back his voice was stern. "Your newspaper doesn't subscribe to AP. This is strictly off the record. Do you understand what that means?" Humbly, I said I did. So he read me the numbers. Next morning, our little weekly had national, state and local election results above the fold on the front page, just like a real newspaper.

One day my editor got word that President Jimmy Carter would speak at the field house in Columbia at noon. "Take your camera and get over there," he barked. I had an hour to make it, so I drove fast, parked illegally, searched for and found the press entrance and joined the line inching up to a table manned by a couple of tough, burly officials. My turn came, and one of them asked for my press pass. I told him I didn't have a pass, but I did have a card. I fumbled to pull out the piece of cardboard that said "Jane Flink, Reporter and Photographer." For extra credit, I flashed the Missouri Highway Patrol ID every journalist gets in the mail, but he just looked at me and shook his head. "Honey," he said, "You can't barge into a presidential speech. Your editor should have applied for clearance a long time ago and they would have mailed your press credentials." I tried to finagle a seat in the farthest corner of the highest balcony, but this was a federal case and it was no dice.

I must have looked pitiful. It was 106 degrees and there was hair and dismay in my eyes. "Tell you what," the tough guy said. "In about an hour the President heads for the airport. If you get out there early, you might get a picture."

I slung my camera bag over my shoulder and spun out for Columbia Regional where I elbowed my way through the crowd till I was close to the fence with its locked gate. The shiny plane was waiting and so was a flock of crew-cut men in three piece suits with wires coming out of their ears. It was 110 degrees on the tarmac but unlike the rest of us, the crew cuts didn't even sweat.

The president's limo pulled up, a deputy sheriff opened the gates and as the crowd flowed through I spotted a great site for a photo. I veered off at a trot, pulling my camera out of the bag bouncing on my hip. When I looked up there were three crew cuts heading my way fast with ugly looks on their faces. At the same time I caught a glimpse of the county sheriff and I yelled "Charley!" The sheriff did a quick take and flashed me a grin, waving off the G-men. Legitimate at last, I got a great shot of President Jimmy Carter waving from the door of Air Force One. The picture ran very small on an inside page in that week's paper. My editor was a Republican.

In 1978 I moved to a Fulton daily newspaper as lifestyles editor where I regularly ripped wire from the Associated Press teletype machine and turned out a couple of eight-page sections every week. Later, as an associate editor at Missouri Ruralist magazine, I spent one week a month on the road in the far reaches of this beautiful state. On assignment for the magazine I rode a cotton picker in the Bootheel, photographed a sodden soybean field under a high Mississippi River levee at floodtide, chronicled the beginnings of big hog operations, carried a pass for the trading floors of the Chicago and Kansas City Boards of Trade and taught an ag-J photography seminar at Kansas State University.

Over a long career I wrote crime news, columns, features, profiles, financial news, medical news, environmental news, government news, editorials and celebrity interviews. One memorable day I stood at the edge of an abyss to photograph the first fuel capsule being lowered into place at the Callaway Nuclear Plant.

When Dick and I bought the *Boone County Journal* we had in mind the recreation of the old *Emporia Gazette*. I wrote thundering editorials about the city council, the county commission, Coke machines in the halls of the new high school and the greedy land-grabbers in the larger city to our north. I held the hands of grieving parents, celebrated with newlyweds and lost sleep over new computer technology. I served on boards and commissions and managed a come-and-go staff. The newspaper was like a Willie Nelson song. It was always on my mind.

Luck is with you when you love your work. For more than 30 years I stitched together the life stories of hundreds of people, operating inside a radius of significant events. When you walk away from the newsroom the world grows quiet. The phones stop ringing, reporter-style wisecracks dry up, the police chief has nothing to tell you, the fax machine goes dead and you wonder where everybody went. I learned fast that nobody cares what you used to be.

For six months after we sold the newspaper, I grieved. For the next six months, like a dog with a bone, I worried a single question: Is there life after journalism? Time tells me there are moments. The county historical society and a bank with a gallery asked me to exhibit my photographs with excerpts from my writing. Lunches with Bruce Wallace, the newspaper's new owner, keep the printer's ink flowing in my veins.

Life after journalism means you can stop building your resume now, take a refresher course in acting like a civilian, discover that the world will turn without your hand on the crank. And convince yourself that it is acceptable just to be.

I said I would never retire, but please, let us define our terms here if we can. If work is a complement to the well-lived life and the ticket to expectation, what is retirement – a rocking chair, or an invitation for self starters? For the moment, I'm holding my own. By nature journalists focus on tomorrow, and life goes on. But do I miss the work I loved all those years? Of course I do, and I always will. Every day of my life.

Small Towns Leave The Light On For You

On a breezy Monday morning in September, most of southern Boone County piled into the Ashland Legion Hall for the annual veterans breakfast. We moved through the food line gathering up steaming plates of biscuits and gravy, scrambled eggs, country ham and sausage. We found a place to sit at the long tables, relaxing into exchanges with hometowners we don't see as often as we would like. As we thanked Legion members for the breakfast, I thought how much I enjoy being part of a small community. And I remembered that it wasn't always like that.

If you ask us, Dick and I will tell you we both come from small towns. His small town was an outpost on the northern border of North Dakota; mine, a suburb of New York City. Neither of them resembles the rural community in central Missouri we were driving toward one chilly evening in 1971. Our family was preparing to move to Centralia where Dick had a new job as plant manager for A. B. Chance, a family-owned international manufacturing company, and I had appointments with real estate agents to find a house for a family of seven.

We were in a sprightly mood as we drove west under the bridges at Kingdom City where Interstate 70 crosses Highway 54 and a scramble of commercial buildings dazzle the night with long-stemmed bouquets of high halogen glare. Right after Kingdom City, we turned sharply north onto a two-lane road. The world went quiet and the night faded to black, spangled by the occasional glimmer of a distant farm security light. We were on a winding blacktop that I would come to know intimately in a few years, but at the moment the darkness felt like a mask forced over my face and I gasped, "Where are you taking me?"

Dick laughed. It was a shortcut, he said. We'd be there soon. And I would love it. But my uneasiness ratcheted up and I was tense with apprehension when 40 minutes later a glow appeared on the horizon and we crossed some railroad tracks, passed a smudge of factory buildings and the shadow of a grain elevator and rolled onto a brightly lit residential street lined with big old houses with wide front porches. "This is my new home," I whispered to myself. Could I learn to love it?

In the past we had followed Dick's career from New York to Milwaukee to Chicago to St. Louis to Burlington, Wisconsin. Like everybody else on the corporate treadmill we'd done plenty of dreaming about leaving the rat race for a job in some peaceful little burg. When A.B. Chance Company came calling with a job offer, it seemed like the answer to a prayer. But like a lot of city and suburban dwellers, I didn't know it takes skill to live in a small Midwestern town. You have to be careful what you pray for.

I found myself one day on the Centralia Square with heavy snow moving in and most of our belongings still crammed into giant moving vans somewhere on the road between Wisconsin and Missouri. When I walked into the local shoe store to buy a pair of boots, I got a welcome that sent me running for cover. "Why hello there, Jane!" said the proprietor, grabbing my hand and pumping it up and down. "We've met Dick and we sure are glad to meet you! Whaddya think of our town? Like to play golf? We've got a great little country club …"

It sounds like a warm welcome. But I wasn't prepared for radical hospitality. I was accustomed to shopping in a cloud of anonymity. Sure, I had favorite retail personnel, but we weren't on a first-name basis and when I left the stores I didn't feel I needed to write a thank-you note. All of a sudden there seemed to be eyes everywhere.

"I'm scared to move!" I wailed to my new friend, Arlene, a Chicago transplant. "I want to hide under the couch. The checkout girl at the grocery store told me she'd see me at the club dance on Saturday night and I don't even know her." Arlene's Centralia exposure was longer than mine. "Time for a reality check," she said. "There's no privacy in a small town. Everybody knows everything you do. Think of it as an extended family," she said. "They'll be there for you if you need them, but they reserve the right to talk about you."

I was frantic to latch on to something familiar. When the *Centralia Fireside Guard* advertised for a part time reporter I leapt at the job. Small town living might be baffling, but writing was something I knew how to do. It was the right move at the right time. The local newspaper provided me with a clinic on small town living, a lifesaver for an outlander who had a lot to learn.

Through my work I met people in their 80s who had been best friends since they started school together. I can't remember the name of anybody in my first grade class. I began to understand why newcomers in a small town are never granted native status. (Next generation, maybe.) I learned the fine line local police walk when their neighbors break the law. came to know that small town doctors harbor a wealth of secrets they never tell, felt the weight of the burdens pastors of all faiths bear in a close-knit community. I learned to be careful what I said to anybody about anybody else. More than likely, they were related.

I learned that small town structures and institutions are not much different from big city models but in a little town everybody knows the players. The editor of the newspaper and the chairman of the city council learn to shelve their differences because they might have to sit side by side in church on Sunday morning, and they wouldn't want to embarrass the children.

I worked four years at the *Guard,* then moved to a daily newspaper south of Kingdom City. To get to work in the morning I drove the same winding country road we followed that black night so many years before. It was familiar territory now. I knew every farmer on the road, every farmer's dog, every piece of farm equipment. I learned to drive with my left hand resting at the top of the steering wheel so I could flip it up in a quick wave when another car passed. In rural Missouri it's rude not to wave when your neighbor goes by in a car. And everybody is your neighbor.

We rented a beautiful old house in Centralia. From there, we built a big brick house on 33 acres south of town where we lived 14 happy years, learning to read the land and interweave its idiom with the history of its people and their habitations, the linkages that make Boone County one large community. When Dick retired from Chance Company, we left the big house with the creek and the woods and the small wild lake. In 1986 we bought the *Boone County Journal* newspaper in the town of Ashland, Missouri (population 1,200) and moved to one of 45 houses nestled in deep woods fronting an 80-acre private lake. The bluffs above the lake overlook the great valley of the Missouri River. Deer and small red foxes come down to the water to drink, and the great blue heron fishes from our cove.

As a country editor in Ashland I had more to learn about reflecting the community's achievements, playing a strong light on tacky little secrets in official places, shamelessly boosting local growth and proofreading till midnight to be sure every name on every page was spelled right.

At the Legion Hall breakfast somebody noted that Dick and I have been hanging around Ashland for more than 15 years now, and I thought how far I had come from those early days in my first rural small town. The briny-sweet country ham paired comfortably with talk about the number of new subdivisions in town and a population nearing 3,000, talk about another family's move to Ashland in the 1950s when strangers "stuck out like a sore thumb," talk about looking at the kids' photos in the newspaper and finding you don't recognize all the names anymore, and of course, talk about each other.

By the time we got to the coffee and the homemade pie, I remembered my friend Arlene's recipe for small town living and concluded she was one wise woman. You know you're at home in a small town when the veterans breakfast is like a family reunion, rich in people you could tell five or six things about, and they could tell the same about you.

Recognition dawned that this day I was living out a twist of fate I couldn't have imagined when I walked into a Centralia shoe store 33 years earlier looking for a pair of boots. When we turned north off the bright Interstate highway into the black night of a rural countryside, we were newcomers, sure to stick out like a couple of sore thumbs. But it's the nature of small town living that newcomer or old hand, you never lose your way because at every turning, somebody leaves the light on for you.

When Canada Geese Made The News

Tom Marshall called me at the Centralia newspaper one warm afternoon in 1975. He said he didn't know, but he might have something I'd like to see. A pair of Canada geese had been coming to his small farm in rural Boone County for several years, the same pair, returning to lay their eggs in the nest Tom had built for them on the farm pond. The goslings had hatched just a few days ago and they were awful cute, Tom said. I told him I was on my way with my camera.

This was about the time the giant Canadas, who had been close to extinction, were beginning to make a comeback. A pair of them, returning to the same small Missouri pond year after year to raise their young, had all the ingredients of a newspaper feature package.

In 1975 nobody could have predicted the rapid increase of the Canada goose in America, or that within a decade, the geese would congregate by the hundreds on golf courses, museum grounds, botanical gardens, and every lake and pond along their flight path.

When we moved to Lake Champetra in 1990, the cheerful barking of the Canadas echoed across the water every winter morning. They cluster in caucuses on the ice that rims spring-fed open water pools. In this new century, wherever there is water and grass, the Canada geese gather in ever-increasing numbers. In Raleigh, N.C., I watched from a lunchroom window at the art museum as squadrons of Canadas marched over a hill on the museum grounds like the pickets of an advancing Confederate army. All this must surely leave conservation professionals in a quandary. In saving the Canada goose from extinction, they undertook a seemingly impossible job and succeeded at it only too well.

There was one winter on our lake when we could set our watches by a flock of Canadas who would circle in from the west every evening at 5 p.m. We would close down the newspaper office a few minutes early, now and then, to be there to hear the geese sentinels barking as they circled, and watch the synchronized splash landing that sent waves swelling across the lake and rippling into our cove.

But all that was tomorrow's news on the day I went out to Tom Marshall's farm to meet his family of geese. We ambled, talking, to the bank where the pond lay still in the sunshine, and settled down in the tall grass to watch. We were on no airline's flight path to anywhere, and except for the land's small creatures rustling and splashing, all was silent. A marmalade kitten crept stealthily down the slope and nestled in my lap and a calf clopped down to the water's edge to drink. The geese vocalized in noisy bursts as they home-schooled their offspring in the two curricula that support their survival – absolute obedience, and learning how to find food.

The Canada goose is a magnificent animal of power and grace, and I used up two rolls of black and white film that day. Tom Marshall, a lean and muscular giant of a man, as gentle as he was tall, loved his geese. He sat beside me in the grass near the tacked-up platform that made a fishing pier jutting out into the water, the kind you see on farm ponds everywhere. The geese seemed to enjoy having an audience, staging air shows, rising with raucous calls to circle the pond and land again with the skidding, feet-first precision you see in baseball runners sliding into second base, cleats high.

I found a stack of the pictures I took that day just about the time controversy began to brew at Lake Champetra over what to do about too many Canada geese. Finding this a pleasant layover in winter, they were making it a year-round home. They invaded the lush green lawns of the homeowners who had rototilled the native undergrowth and rolled out expanses of sod at lakeside. Understandably, these homeowners were not liking what the visiting geese left behind.

As I looked through the pictures, remembering Tom Marshall's pride in the family of Canadas that came home every year, my neighbors were searching Department of Conservation literature, looking for ways to be sure these latter-day geese move on when winter is over.

At our house we can afford to be philosophical about the geese. They don't trespass on our land at the lake because we leave our yard in a natural wooded state and there is nothing here that a goose wants, no emerald swath meeting the water's edge. We wait for the early native wildflowers to die back in spring before we weed whip for neatness and snake control. As a result, we are as fond of the Canada geese as we are of the great blue heron who fishes in our cove, or the elusive red foxes who venture down from the upland woods to hunt the lakeshore.

I can't imagine Canada geese as the subject of a full-page photo feature in any newspaper in America today, unless it is a study of what a plague they've become. Yet making room for a mother and father goose and their goslings in classrooms would teach children everything they need to know about family values. Canada geese mate for life and are far more devoted than their human observers to raising good kids. On a country road one day a father goose saw my car as a threat to his brood and with no hesitation, protecting his family, took on the car itself, flying closely beside me for a mile, barking insults and lunging at the window.

Driving cross county my heart lifts at the sight of the great V formations Canadas string across the sky. I seek out the homely welcome of their winter morning barks, the chatter and ruffling of feathers in a settling flock's noisy splashdown that's not unlike a bevy of passengers deplaning from a 747.

Years ago a Boone County farmer introduced me to a family of Canada geese and the compelling majesty of these big birds still fills me with awe. The Canada goose teetered on the brink of extinction and was saved by conservationists who didn't know how successful they could get. Rebounding in large numbers, geese have become aliens in a world of shopping malls and too many people. Yet for all their numbers I find myself wishing that the life of a Canada goose could be always wild and free, and not in the least newsworthy.

The Newsroom Chili Wars

The ceilings were high in the old concrete building that housed *The Kingdom Daily Sun-Gazette* in Fulton, Missouri. When I worked there in the late 1970s, the newsroom was big, open, full of desks and ringing telephones, and it had never seen the services of an interior designer. When the sports guy looked up from his typewriter he might encounter the glazed eyes of the feisty young female newshound seeking inspiration from the pipes that ran down the wall behind his desk.

When a phone rang, everybody listened and useless advice and scurrilous suggestions flew back and forth. The place was, in fact, a madhouse full of constant talk, where hard decisions were made in a nanosecond and we breathed the air of our shared creativity and bounced ideas from desk to desk. When deadlines neared, everybody hunkered down and the room went quiet except for the furious clacking of typewriter keys.

Spartan as the newsroom was, I felt that I was leaving sanctuary in the four winters I worked there when I had to drive my 45-minute commute at midnight in a howling snowstorm. The most navigable roads were highway 54 through Mexico, then highway 22 to Centralia. The most hazardous spot was a long slope downhill to Mexico where cars slid helplessly sideways, all of the drivers praying hard. Rival hazard filled the miles closest to home when I turned off blacktop to drive uphill on gravel. On really bad nights I hoped only to get my car within walking distance of our house in the country. When the car wouldn't make it I slogged through snowdrifts the rest of the way on frozen feet.

I was the oldest person in the newsroom and as lifestyles editor, I took a lot of heat from the hard news purists. The boys wanted me to play Mom but I told them I'd been there, done that. I said I took the job to see what *Animal House* was really like. In fact, most of the kids I worked with were setting high goals for themselves, laying the groundwork for big jobs they would hold in the future. The challenge that spurred me on was the change in the lifestyles sections of daily newspapers. They were moving away from society news to universal issues like the influx of women into the workplace, clean air and water, the need for renewable energy resources and progress in medicine.

In slack moments our work-related intensity took a holiday. Things could get rowdy. A reporter covered the story of a drunk found sleeping on the sidewalk in his underwear and he polled the newsroom on what we wore to bed. I don't have to describe the conversation – your imagination will take you everywhere that raucous hubbub went. We were toting up the results, uncovering the fact that half the staff slept in their underwear, when a very pretty girl from advertising walked through the room. "Hey," one of the reporters yodeled. "Do you sleep in your underwear?" She glared, flipped her hair and stalked out while everybody applauded. Then a phone rang and the typewriters started up again.

Each of us took a turn editing the weekend edition so the editor could take a break. It was his job to select front page news and work with the composing people on the layout of the front section. I had the drill down pat and my section put to bed when the newsroom emptied out. The place was quiet except for the chattering of the AP teletype and the ominous creaks and groans of an old building talking to itself.

I was working through the routine when the "big story" bell rang on the wire. Why me, I growled, reading the nightmare news that Three Mile Island nuclear power plant had erupted. Big stories like that one start out small and grow as the details fill in, so you ignore the chills running up your spine and push deadline to the last possible minute to get as much information into the paper as you can. We countered in following editions of the paper with in-depth reports on the Callaway

Nuclear Plant under construction near the Fulton community, all of us full of the coursing adrenaline news people thrive on. A vocal group of townspeople were spooked by the close proximity of nuclear power and that first week we braced ourselves for a big reader reaction to the Three Mile Island story, but it never happened.

The chili wars began that week. I was putting together a food page for the lifestyles section and found Elizabeth Taylor's favorite chili recipe. The news editor got hold of it first. He was from Texas and he howled so loud heads swiveled. "You don't put tomatoes in chili," he yelled. "Chili is chuck wagon food. Where do you think those ol' boys got tomatoes on a cattle drive?" This wasn't getting by our California reporter. "Chile wasn't invented on cattle drives," she snorted. "It was an old Mexican dish. They grew tomatoes." The sports guy said no tomatoes and no beans in real chili. You cut up beef and onions and stew them all day with red peppers. It's the peppers that turn the chili red. "You gotta have beans," said the photographer.. "In old Mexico they put beans in everything. What you don't want is ground beef. Putting ground beef in chili is like putting ketchup on apple pie."

Scenting a reader pleaser, I was scribbling a page layout as fast as I could and I made all of them type up their chili recipes and sign their names to them. When our special chili page came out we got letters and phone calls and before long everybody in town was talking about staging a chili cook-off.

Just down the road Union Electric had assembled a public relations army ready to assure Callawegians that their nuclear power plant would be immune to the sort of thing that happened at Three Mile Island. Back at our shop, the talk about how to make the perfect pot of chili gained heat as it grew. We never heard much about the danger of a nuclear meltdown right in our backyard. Later there was plenty of nuclear anxiety, but right after Three Mile Island our readers were up to their necks in chili recipes. There's no explaining it. That's just the way it is, sometimes, in the newsroom.

Once A Reporter...

I started writing about Missouri agriculture at a time when interest rates were sky high and farm prices dismally low. In the early 1980s, *Missouri Ruralist* magazine hired me as an assistant editor. On my travels around the state in search of stories, I found plenty of misery. Farm families were going broke, being forced out of their homes, losing the land and the lifestyle they loved. They had followed the best advice from departments of agriculture, universities, chemical companies, farm magazines and equipment dealers. They had leveraged everything, and now they were going under. As a veteran reporter, I believed the downturn in the farm economy was a major news story. The magazine didn't see it that way.

The corporate owners in Ohio, the ones who had our paychecks mailed from Orlando, had the final say, and they were taking the long view. They had accepted that small farms in America were history. They wanted stories about big farm operations run by producers with an eye to a productive future.

On my route, change was everywhere, demonstrated by soybean producers turning their acreage into U-pick fruit and vegetable farms, by Centennial farms that gussied up picturesque barns and filled them with homemade crafts and home-grown produce, turning them into wayside country stores. Counseling centers moved into northern Missouri to help farm families living shattered lives in a broken economy. NPR ran with that story. We didn't.

Alcoholism was growing among farmers and spousal abuse was on the rise. Willie Nelson took his show on the road in support of farm families who were losing land that had been passed down for generations. Small towns boarded up their buildings. Without income from agriculture to bankroll the feed stores, sales lots and local businesses, whole communities shut down. At the apex of irony, in the early 1980s farmers began applying for food stamps.

From all over the Midwest, Missouri included, angry farmers fueled up their tractors and formed a cavalcade bound for Washington D.C., desperately seeking help for a farm economy gone haywire. These were the stories I wanted to tell and occasionally my editor would shake his head and say, "Once a reporter …" and he would let me write something he knew would bring a blistering rebuke from headquarters.

In spite of the restrictions, I was glad the Ruralist let me work there. I had come on board with no background in ag journalism. I kept a stiff upper lip when my editor told me my beat would be the U.S. legislature and the farm economy, one column on each subject for every issue in addition to my feature work. It was my job to make it clear what Washington was up to before it rained down on every farmer's south forty. But I had plenty to be glad about. Before long, the magazine promoted me to associate editor and raised my salary.

There were four writer/photographer/editors on our team and we divided up the state of Missouri, each of us spending one week of every month on the road, gathering information and photographs, coming back with notebooks full of stories and rolls of exposed film. We would hole up alone in some small motel and depend on extension agents, word of mouth, weekly newspapers and local farmers for our sources. Back at the office we processed black and white film and handed dozens of color slides to our editor, hoping he would choose one of ours for a cover. Then we sat at our computers, wrote our stories and sent them by telephone to a mainframe in Duluth, Minnesota where the magazine was assembled.

Knowing I needed instruction in the finer points of farm finance and methods, I looked for guidance to the ag professors at the University of Missouri-Columbia. They laughed at my gaffes, took me to lunch, described their world with precision and answered all my questions. If I looked up "thank you" in every dictionary in every language on earth, it wouldn't be "gracias" enough for all they taught me. I used what I learned when I booked motel rooms in Sikeston and Sedalia and Cuba and Maryville, spending a week interviewing cotton and rice growers, row croppers, cow/calf operators or big pork producers. After a couple of years, I elevated the Steelville area to my top spot among the most beautiful landscapes in Missouri.

In 1985 I was offered a job as director of the Winston Churchill Memorial and Library at Westminster College where I would blend my love of writing with my devotion to history. A few years after I left, the farm magazine was sold and under new owners, it fell on hard times, the victim of a downturn in the industry that reflected the hard times farmers endured in the early 1980s.

The 80s never really went away. Between 1980 and 2006, the percentage of farmers in the U.S. population dropped by half, and many of those remaining on the land are involved in some type of corporate farming. Corporate farming was what most farmers feared as they told me through their tears what the family farm used to be and all that it had meant to them.

My years at the *Ruralist* were rich with events. I flew to Reno to photograph the new tractor produced by a merger of two major equipment companies. I was there when the brilliant red machine rose from the stage in a cloud of multicolor smoke and thousands of farmers and dealers jumped to their feet and cheered. With my editor, I attended a garden party at the White House hosted by President Reagan in honor of agricultural journalists. On a trip to Missouri's Bootheel I studied new methods of growing cotton, rode in the high cab of a state-of-the-art cotton picker and from there flew east to tour the headquarters of Cotton Incorporated in Raleigh, North Carolina. The next stop was New York City where, in a sleek showroom overlooking Central Park, the cotton fabrics of the season were unveiled for designers to choose their palettes two years in advance.

One snowy evening our magazine staff had cocktails at the Yacht Club on Lake Michigan before dinner on the floor of the Chicago Board of Trade. I was one of a group invited to serve on the Governor's Task Force investigating horse racing in Kentucky.

Given such a wealth of good things – the education, the people, the travel – I still felt guilty about the human misery that walked side by side with the decline of the family farm. And so I moved on.

There are certain absolutes that reporters owe to their readers. Among them are truth, integrity, empathy and accuracy. My editor wanted me to stay, but he understood staffers with inner turmoil. He shook his head and said it again: "Once a reporter…" And I would be the last reporter to say he was wrong.

Old Songs Go Round and Round

Does anybody sing the old songs anymore? Do kids gather around campfires when the stars are out on black summer nights, hugging their knees, their faces burnished by the firelight and begin to sing, "There's a long, long trail a-winding, into the land of my dreams…" or "Smile the while you bid me fond adieu…" or "I had a dream, dear; you had one too…?"

Everybody used to know those old songs and everybody sang them, songs that echoed the joys and sorrows of a time long before we were born, lazy melodies and soft harmonies and the sweet sad words that lulled us into reverie after sunlit days at camps in the woods and clambakes on the beach and church picnics and school outings.

We sang the songs our parents knew when they were young in World War I – "Give My Regards to Broadway," and "Over There" and "My Gal Sal." How did we learn them? There wasn't one of us alive when those songs were written but these were the songs we sang around the campfires. Does anybody sing them anymore?

Without consciously memorizing them, I know the words to more than one lifetime of songs, so many that when I slip in a disc or turn the radio dial to pick up music to write by, the words of the songs intrude and scramble my thoughts. No matter what keys my fingers are brushing,

I'm thinking about what comes after "Fools rush in, where angels fear to tread…"

When I began full-time work as a journalist I realized that I approach writing in a way that may not be usual; that is, the words come first. I treasure the quirky turn of a phrase, my own or someone else's. I relish the roll of vowels, the chirrup of diphthongs, powerful cusswords, colorful slang and the twanging subjunctive.

I trap thoughts and seek tales to tell because the words have come and cry out to be used. Words that allow me to massage the language, making sentences and non-sentences to create a hum, a rhythm, a cadence that forms a piece of work that says something. The words are the message as well as the messengers, their form and shape, their taste on the back of the tongue, their resonance in the ear, put down on paper. Words put to music arrive pre-cadenced, cleverly crafted for insertion into our memory banks.

The songs go round and round the generations. Songs that were hits when I was a teenager are classics now. Even when I'm hearing an instrumental rendition I silently sing along: "My funny Valentine…" or "I've got the world on a string, sittin' on a rainbow, got the string around my finger…" Or "Unforgettable – that's what you are." Or "When the deep purple falls, over sleepy garden walls, and the stars begin to glimmer in the sky; in the mist of a memory you wander back to me, breathing my name with a sigh…"

What is it about music? Ask me to memorize a passage from a book and I'll tell you memorization isn't one of my talents. But set that passage to music and play it a few times and I'll never forget it. "Rally Round the Flag, Boys" and "When Johnny Comes Marching Home" date back to the Civil War. "Don't Sit Under the Apple Tree" comes from World War II, "Who's Sorry Now" from the 50s, "Morning Has Broken" from the 60s, "You Needed Me" came along in the 70s, and somewhere the ageless melancholy blues took root in my heart, songs like "Nobody Knows the Troubles I've Seen."

Pop music has always thrown out a variety of sounds and nobody really knows why some of it stays around and some of it fades away like the fitful wind of a blustery day. There's a wealth of new music out there, but the charts lost me when rap arrived. Musicologists tell me rap is a legitimate art form, but is there really music there, and more to the beat than a repetition of "uh (pause, pause) and uh uh (pause) and are the words that should rhyme not rhyming on purpose, or is the whole thing a mistake like the Emperor's clothes?

Maybe everybody reaches a critical stage when the old songs have more appeal than the new ones, and maybe that's where I am now. But it cheers me to know that I'm not entirely alone. My grandchildren are mad for Frank Sinatra and it's as common as dirt to punch up one of many electronic devices and still hear, "Embrace me, you sweet embraceable you… or "Night and day, you are the one…" or "Straighten up and fly right…"

That last one – that's what I want to do when I'm writing a newspaper column. You would think I'd have learned that there are a lot of things you can do to music, but writing isn't one of them. Writing blossoms in the fertility of silence. So I straighten up and turn off the radio or lift the disc where the lyrics trap awareness and the music goes round and round.

It's All About Light

That Sunday was a come-again, go-again sort of day, the sun in and out of a general overcast, a good kind of day for a show of my black and white photography at the Montminy Gallery in Columbia, Missouri. People came and looked at the show and toured the adjacent county museum, local families at odds and ends on the final day of the Thanksgiving holiday and visitors from other states turning off the highway to stretch their legs. Light poured into the breezeway between the museum and the art gallery – that slightly diffused overcast light photographers treasure above all others, the light that casts a silver sheen on everything it touches, a holy grail sort of light, the answer to a photographer's prayer.

The photos in the show are mine, Missouri people and places from the decade 1975 to 1985, pictures shot when I was writer/photographer/editor at the *Centralia Fireside Guard* newspaper, lifestyles editor at the *Kingdom Daily Sun-Gazette* and associate editor of *Missouri Ruralist* magazine. Each of the photographs was published as part of a story or maybe an enterprise shot to liven up a page, like the picture of the housewife walking her cat early one morning. The woman is wearing a distant, sleepy expression above a rumpled housecoat, the cat stretching his leash to its ultimate length, every muscle knit in rebellion.

On Sunday afternoon the light in the breezeway details each petal of a dozen white roses on the reception table, falls like a filmy veil over platters of food. A bright day casts strong, defining shadows but a slight overcast makes you see things newly and as they are. Waiting for people to arrive I pace, thinking I would rather be boiled in oil than stand for two hours wearing a sign that reads "Artist." Inside the gallery, each photograph is lighted, each labeled, each telling its own story, distancing me from them, making me feel my presence an intrusion. I had been there at the beginning of them and now, I think, I ought to go away and let these my children speak for themselves. But when people come, walking slowly from photo to photo, studying them, the images introduce viewer and photographer, bring us together through memory, technique, nostalgia, commentary. The pure gold I bring away from the show is the phrase I hear repeated, "The pictures touched my heart."

The photo show happened because museum and gallery director Deborah Slade Thompson saw a few of my photos and asked if I would do a show and I said sure and the idea floated through the spring and summer and then we set a date and when Sunday came I was pacing the gallery floor in the presence of this now-slightly-alien work of my hands neatly displayed on clean white walls.

The value of the exhibit is not that it represents great art or even great photography but that the images reflect the hands-on technology of a past decade, a way of working that still exists but is confined in a digital age to purists and artists. Late 20th century photojournalists chose camera, film, chemicals, paper, exposure and timing and bent them to their liking, creating photographs that manifested personal style. Printing done today by computer was then a product of the darkroom and a number of gallery guests spoke longingly of darkrooms, those dungeons of half light that swallow time, places where image fills your brain, directs your hands, suffuses space. Places where red light and clean chemical smells seem to seep into your pores, separate you from yourself, merge you with the creative process.

I am struck by the symmetry of the images on the gallery walls, as simple and ordered as Quaker dress, recalling how they languished for 20 years in ill-sorted stacks in basement storerooms. That they survived at all is something of a miracle. How many times I told myself to chuck these useless relics of a past life; after all, I had tossed hundreds of other photos into piles in newsrooms to be stuffed into trash bins. Journalists focus on tomorrow.

 I set these few aside because they were good enough to enter contests and most of them went on to win awards. And then I couldn't let them go because they kept on telling me stories: the sweet, pensive face of a young bride in her wedding finery; a homeless man with his bottle at his side sleeping against a warm brick wall in early spring sunshine; a pair of strict women, good women, pillars of their community, ladies of the club; a farm family facing hard times.

During the 1970s and '80s I taught photography at workshops around the state. Mostly I taught training the eye to see and assess light. In black and white photography it's the light that matters and how you make use of it as it falls on the face or the object or the landscape. Light in its varying intensities produces shadow, and light and shadow together reveal the image we call a photograph, so it's not so much the face that matters, or the object, or the landscape. In the end result, all that matters is the light.

The photographs were on exhibit there for five months and I came back and looked at them and did interviews about them with media people. The images are clean and clear and simple; it isn't a complicated sort of show, just a collection from a working journalist that focuses attention on Missouri and Missourians. It's art, yes, but it isn't big art and it isn't the art that matters so much as it is the form and texture of the history, the stories the pictures tell us of how we lived in the last quarter of the century just past, and who lived there with us and what sort of light all that brought into our lives.

CREATIVE TOOLS

Some years ago, in a rural town in Callaway County, I met a man who was a woodcarver. He was middle-aged, dark-haired and lean and he had trouble breathing, stopping between words to suck in air as he told me his story. He had worked most of his life at another trade and he had smoked cigarettes until his lungs gave out and he was forced to retire. He came home to his wife, to their small neat house in a clearing in the woods, and he began to work with fallen branches, carving little statues of animals and birds and later, in the bark of selected split logs, he carved the faces he found there.

The faces looked the way woodfolk should, roughhewn with intense or wistful eyes. He told me he didn't approach a bit of wood with any notion of what he would carve. As he worked, the image that was in the wood appeared to him and all he had to do was set it free. He tilted his head back and looked at the stands of trees around his house and paused to take a breath for talking and said he wished he could see all the images that were out there.

All of us harbor a creative gene. We have always made images of fellow creatures, landscapes and cloudscapes, created music and dance and drama choosing random instruments to reproduce reality or summon spirit worlds. Artists speak of the presence of the finished work in the pages they write on, in the canvas they paint, in the paint itself or the clay they use and acknowledge that the goal of the artist is to release what is already there – the beauty, the powerful statement, the image that engages the hearts and minds of humankind.

To write stories is to take your thoughts and throw them yo-yo fashion into the vast unknown to see what comes back, to dig deep inside dark places in the corners of your mind for cobwebs of insight and memory, to force random thoughts, capers of humor and all your sensibilities into a frame bound by words, on a page defined by sensibilities of its own.

When we attest that pencil, paint and paper, clay, the computer screen, the land where the house will be built, the arc in the air the dancer's foot will trace, are themselves creative, we are not speaking of negative space in painting or sculpture or architecture – the "blanks" that define composition – but something as ephemeral and at the same time as concrete as the faces hidden in the wood.

Rosamond Bernier wrote of her friendship with the painter, Miro, who loved old brushes, those that were uneven and flattened out, because they produced unexpected results, accidents on the canvas. Old brushes, he said, had lived, had lives of their own.

Writer Annie Dillard exalts the blank page: "Who will teach me to write?" a reader asks and she responds: "... the page, that eternal blankness... which you cover slowly, affirming time's scrawl as a right and your daring as necessity, the page, which you cover woodenly, ruining it, but asserting your freedom and power to act, acknowledging that you ruin everything you touch but touching it nevertheless, because acting is better than being here in mere opacity... the page in the purity of its possibilities... against which you pit such flawed excellences as you can muster with all your life's strength: that page will teach you to write."

The limitless creative makes us disposed to meld with our medium, acknowledging its power over the work we call our own, to *become* the process. "Remember that you are created creative," says poet Maya Angelou, surrounded by all creation and in every creative act part of the creative whole, of the page and the canvas and the clay and in humility, uncomfortably, one with the Great Creator. All creativity puts us in touch with the mind of God, even setting out tomato plants in our gardens. We create, find our creation unworthy, smash it, do this over and over till an image satisfies. Creativity is a gift, is an explosion of sharing across impenetrable barriers. It will blind you at times, and make you deaf, and take you and shake you and drag you through dark places to the heights of isolated pinnacles and abandon you there.

It's easier to imagine the house on the land than the face in the wood or the words inherent on a page or a shape defined in air for a balletomane to trace. In fact the medium is the message, in part is the work itself – there is poetry in the pen, a masterpiece in the brush, music in the small black symbols ranked in a ruled notebook. Who can deny the link between creator and creative tools? Lacking their power, symbolism fails us, metaphor unravels and the dancer's foot, so impeccably shod, probes aimlessly in the air.

Chapter Two: Learning from Living

THE DEEP END

The experience is familiar but that doesn't take the fear out of it, living temporarily in a passage of your life where you can't see a straight path from here to there, where your destination is clouded and you can't adequately define what "there" is.

It happens at the end of high school and college, that feeling of stepping off into the deep end. It happens when a couple stands before a minister or priest or a rabbi and one or both of them recognizes something inside that warns them to hold up, back off, return to the familiar. It happens when people retire, when they move from one place to another, sell furniture and collections, draw room plans on graph paper, walk through strange houses they might buy, aware that nobody can tell how a house will live no matter how many times you visit it, draw it, imagine it.

On summer days when I was six years old I would walk with my friends to the municipal pool in my New Jersey home town. The pool was actually a small lake with an island at one end where people tied up their kayaks and canoes and held picnics in the sunshine.

We changed into bathing suits in shelter houses above a wide crescent of sandy beach that sloped gently into shallow water where little kids played. Beyond a line of floats was the deep end where only practiced swimmers were allowed. If a kid my age approached the floats the lifeguard would shrill his whistle and everybody would assume an innocent face. "It wasn't *me*," said the faces turned earnestly toward the lifeguard's stand.

Sitting on the beach with towels around our shoulders we would talk about the deep end and what was likely to be out there. We summoned up water monsters, giant snakes, prehistoric turtles that would grab your toes and drag you down into dark oblivion and we would shiver in unison, as if a cold wind swept along the crescent of beach that hot summer day. Someone said drowning was a happy death because just before the end the victim thinks, "Oh it's okay – I can breathe water!" and then… blackness. The deep end of our municipal pool was as unknown as love and death.

There is nothing we can do about our age at any given time and there was nothing I could ever do about my father who was an elemental force like lightning, prone to strike almost anywhere. Inevitably I turned seven and my father decided it was time for me to learn to swim.

On this instance he struck in a startling way, accompanying us one day to the pool where he swam casually to the deep end, rested awhile, then came to get me where I was playing in the shallows. I laughed when he towed me out to the far raft, the one in the deepest part of the deep end, and showed me how to climb the ladder. Then he picked me up and threw me into the water. I went down, down, down and down, into the murky depths; then, to my surprise, I began to rise and cleared water barking like a seal and paddling like a dog toward the raft where my father stood in the sunshine. "Good!" he said. And he dove into the deep water, swam to the shore and went home, his mission accomplished.

Throwing a kid into deep water to teach her how to swim was accepted practice when I was a child and there is a certain logic in it. Dogs, cats, assorted rodents and people, tossed into water, call on instinct and paddle, a practice that supports survival. Later I was given swimming lessons. But I learned some things about the deep end from that first dunking. I learned that my father trusted me to take care of myself. I learned that water will hold you up, that there's a Zen experience in the caress of deep water on bare limbs. And I learned that the deep end was not what I thought it was. It was much more dangerous than that.

For most of my life I swam and surfed in the cold, turbulent Atlantic Ocean and from my earliest days I always knew that I would rather swim than eat. After I'd been slammed flat by high surf and dragged along a broken-shell strand by a strong undertow I learned never to turn my back on the waves.

In a large, cold lake in New York State, when our small boat died, a friend and I jumped in the water to push the boat back to shore. We learned that boats sit very high in the water and there are no handholds. It was a long swim but not as long as the day we dared each other to swim the width of the lake and found what it was like after the first mile to be very, very tired in the water when nobody else knows where you are. Found how deep within we had to reach to keep counting, keep breathing, keep stroking, keep calm and allow the water to keep us afloat. Discovered that at the end, when we were within yards of the shore, we were unashamed to resort to frantic dog paddling.

Deep end experiences mark our lives like stars pasted in our workbooks – the sudden loss of a job and its income, graduations, weddings, divorces, resettlements, challenges we take on because we choose to, even military call-ups can cloud our outlook like the veiled gravity of deep water.

But we have experience to call on and it tells us to persevere, to keep the count, breathe deeply, stay calm, and when we must, dog paddle as hard as we can to the raft, to the shore, to the safe place where we can sit together in the sunshine on a crescent beach with towels around our shoulders, sharing hair-raising stories of the dangers of the deep and our own undaunted courage.

Shadow Selves At Your Service

A friend asked me recently about the health and well being of my shadow selves. I had to confess, regretfully, that if I had any, our relationship has been so slight that I might have sat on them thinking they were cushions. Now that she mentioned it, I'm finding shadow selves in my past and in my future – the young mother and homemaker with the efficient schedule; the untaught painter who brush stroked a Wisconsin winter in bold colors; the journalist, assertive and ever present; the publisher with pride of ownership; the photographer, making a comeback as art sidesteps technology and embraces light in silver gelatin prints.

I tried recently to conjure up a shadow self, one with a jaunty attitude and a cocky grin. I was flunking the MRI exam my doctor needed to diagnose a dysfunctional shoulder and I was ready to deliver a lateral pass to any shadow self willing to catch it.

I was fine, I thought, when I followed the technician into the room with the big machine and lay down on the gliding slab that could have been something fancy from a mausoleum. The technician told me the MRI would define the damage causing the pain in my shoulder and asked me if that was okay and I said, not really. And she said are you claustrophobic? And I said yes. So she talked some more and began easing the slab and the patient (me, head first, face up) under the big machine that covers half the room and I thought, "Crikey, my nose isn't going to clear."

By the time about half your body is in position the machine is a scant two inches over your face, and I started to shake and couldn't stop and a headline appeared on the inside of my forehead foreshadowing doom: "50,000 pound machine props fail; MRI a killer," my shadow headline read. And then the catch line in smaller type: "Death not instantaneous; firemen unsuccessful in rescue attempt."

No amount of skilled intervention stopped the shaking so the tech slid me out and we both tried to persuade me to try again and failed. I had to make an appointment to try again the next day under the influence of 10 grams of valium from my pharmacist. When you live in a small town the pharmacist will get a big kick out of your 10 grams of valium and give you a hard time about it, so I was feeling like a disgraced military officer who showed the white feather in combat and became an object of contempt and derision.

The nice technician told me she has "a person like me" about once a week – you are or you're not claustrophobic, she said, and there's not a whole lot you can do about it. Then she smiled and told me about the big guy who shook like a cement mixer and she had to slide him out of the machine. He stood up and said if it was all right with her he'd be back in a couple of hours ready to try again and she said actually, she had some time open. When he came back he was easy with it. "You're sure you're going to make it this time?" she asked, arranging him on the slab. "Absolutely," he said with a beatific smile. "Two martinis will do it every time."

I drove my failed self home in heavy traffic through thunderstorms and dragged into the house, convinced my shadow selves had let me down. "How did it go?" Dick asked. "It didn't go," I said. "I feel just the way I felt the day I flunked my Latin final in seventh grade." So he said soothing things and I told him that was fine but he would have been brave enough to do it and he said I couldn't know that till he tried and he wasn't in a hurry to try. "Why don't you just relax and have a martini?" he said.

The closest I came to a heart-to-heart with a shadow self was when I was a young journalist shooting photos for feature stories. There were three things I knew about photography: one, all a black and white film does is capture light and shadow; two, to do really good work you have to carry a camera with you every day until it becomes an extension of your arm; and three, there is an indefinable connection that springs up between photographer and subject (whether the subject is a person or a building or a tree) and it's only when you feel that shadow self take hold and let it guide you that good work results, photographs with a certain sheen to them, a gloss that isn't possible if the link isn't there.

Recently I have shown some of those now-historic photos in gallery exhibits. The photographer shadow was a welcome self because she stilled the noise in my head. Writers "see" in words and if their lives are eventful the words stack up fast, not like clothes in the attic but like four radio stations playing all at one time. The only resort is to sit down and write the noise out of your head. Or switch to the other half of your brain and pick up a paint brush or a camera so you can live in a medium where instead of writing *about* something you *become* something, one with that person, that building, that tree.

Shadow selves, once recognized, have a way of multiplying. The homemaker, the painter, the journalist, the publisher, the photographer, all are tempered for my instruction. An old song recalls a time when "the quiet shadows falling, softly come and softly go." On their own terms, shadow selves move through our lives like that, recalling who we used to be, defining who we are, forecasting with more courage than we could manage by ourselves the persons we are destined to become.

Always Lie About Your Age

Over the last quarter century I never thought much about my age. Maybe that's why the need to retire came as such a surprise. Day followed week followed month and the years slipped by. I was on a roll and not paying attention.

It was different in the first third of my life. I thought about my age most of the time then. I was the youngest in my family and the youngest in my class and I was always playing catch-up, so when age became an issue I pretended I was older.

When I was four, I told my first lie. I said I was five. It was a matter of *omerta*. Everybody else in my gang was five and I couldn't embarrass them. Gang warfare had erupted in Marietta, Georgia. A bunch of kids from another neighborhood were daring us to cross the street our parents said we couldn't cross. The forbidden street was a lifesaver – we made faces, threw pebbles and yelled yah, yah, yah, knowing we were safe. They weren't allowed to cross the street either.

When I was 13 I told people I was almost 15. I was reprimanded once for telling an employer that I was 21 when I was only 20. I was applying for a great job and I wanted it badly. I'd forgotten that Cold War ID requirements meant my fingerprints, blood type and birth certificate were all on file. The personnel manager could have fired me on the spot, but instead he thought it was funny. "You're the only woman I ever met who said she was older when she lied about her age," he said, and sent me back to my office. Then he told the story to everybody in the building.

My first indication that I was aging arrived one morning as I was boarding a Philadelphia trolley that would take me to my great new job. A crush of high school kids was rushing the door. Suddenly one of them yelled, "Hey! Make room for the lady!" I looked around for the lady and realized they were talking about me. I was wearing a suit, stockings and high heels and anyway, by then I was really 21.

Age is almost always relative to something. Humorist George Carlin said you *become* 21, *turn* 30, *push* 40, *reach* 50, *make it* to 60 and *hit* 70. Once you get into your 80s, he said, you *hit* lunch, *turn* 4:30 and *reach* bedtime. By the time you're 100, you go back to exaggerating your age the way you did as a child. "I'm 100 and a half!" old folks brag.

You don't realize it's your age that's the problem when you first begin to wonder how come this country is turning everything over to a bunch of kids who have no manners and couldn't possibly know the ropes.

"Hello, Edith," your new doctor says, sticking out his hand. "I'm Dr. Sawbucks." Dr. Sawbucks has pink cheeks that have never seen a razor. Not only does this boy-child want you to take off your clothes, he calls you by your first name, showing he has no respect for his elders. Young doctors ask questions that sound like they came out of a *Parade* magazine quiz. "On a scale of one to 10, how do you rate your pain?" If Edith has any sense she'll remember the doctor's full name – Cash Sawbucks. When she leaves she'll stick out her hand and say, "Thanks, Cash. On a scale of one to 10, I'd rate this office visit a three."

My husband hates to go to the doctor, even a doctor he likes as a person. That's because doctors tell him what to do and he hates being told what to do. Doctors write prescriptions that command, "Take 3 mg on Tuesday and Thursday, 4 on Monday and Wednesday and call me on Friday." Dick reads the doctors' instructions with steam coming out of his ears.

I never tell my husband what to do. I just bring the telephone directory to the breakfast table. "What're you looking for?" he asks over his coffee cup. "Oh, just a man to clean out the gutters," I say. "Gutters!" he says. "You want to pay somebody to clean out the gutters? I'm certainly not too old to clean out my own gutters!" Now all you have to do is say sweetly, "Here, let me give you a hand with that ladder."

My mother always said no woman with any sense ever tells her age because nobody is going to believe her. The people who think of her as older will whisper, "She's lying, of course." The people who think of her as younger will gasp, "I didn't know she was *that* old!" If you go around telling your age, she said, the day will come when somebody will use it against you.

Our youngest son knew about relative ages when he was five years old. Turning five is almost as important as being 21. One morning I told him to do something and he asked why he had to do it and I explained he had to do it because I was his mother and I was older than he was.

He thought about the subject of age according to the numbers he knew. "Are you six?" he asked. Older than six, I said. "Well, are you 10?" Older even than 10, I told him. "Say," he said. "Just how old are you, anyway?" "Actually, I'm 35," I said. His eyes widened and he stared at the floor. "Well," he said, "You're big for your age."

I reached out and ruffled that little tow head, this child, blood of my blood, bone of my bone, and reflected that my mother was right. When it comes to your age, forget about telling the truth. There's nobody in this world you can trust.

When Charlie Ravioli Came To Town

It's Monday morning and I'm recovering from a major holiday, a two-week vacation, and confronting a home office tangled in busyness and miscommunication. E-mails are going astray. My telephone answering machine started picking up on the second ring, sending callers scurrying to get out of its way. This is not retirement as advertised. Calling retail firms, I get cyborgs telling me to "Press 1," enter the department number, the password, my Social Security number, my date of birth, the seven-digit code.

Do I have a seven-digit code? There's nobody to ask. "Please!" I think. "Where did all the real people go?"

We used to stop by and see each other, write letters to friends and family. When I was a child there was a simple black telephone handset that nested in its cradle on a plain black stand in the foyer of our house. In the center of the stand was a small white oval with our telephone number stamped there – RIdgewood 6-1185. When you picked up the handset a telephone operator with a pleasant voice said, "Number, please." You told the operator the number and she did the work.

Some time ago I clipped from a *New Yorker* magazine the tale of an imaginative child and a telephone of a different kind. It's a captivating story by Adam Gopnik about his three-year-old daughter Olivia who lives in a New York apartment with her busy parents and her Fisher Price telephone. Olivia isn't concerned about real people; she has an imaginary playmate named Charlie Ravioli. Olivia's friend works "on a television" and he is never there when she wants him to come out and play. "Okay," Olivia says to her phone. "Call me. Bye." When Olivia calls Charlie, she says, she always gets his machine.

In her imagination Olivia bumps into Charlie Ravioli and they have coffee or grab lunch. Then they hail a cab because Ravioli always has to run. The author is worried about the little girl's pretend friend and calls his sister, a California psychologist. The sister tells him the imaginary playmate is perfectly normal. As for the lifestyle Olivia has adopted, the sister-psychologist suggests it's time for Gopnik to pack his bags and move his family to the country.

But you and I know the country isn't the answer. In this small town in the Midwest we hear our own voices when the author asks his wife how her day went. "Oh, you know," Martha says. "I tried to make a date with Meg, but I couldn't find her, so I left a message on her machine. Then I bumped into Emily after that meeting... and we had coffee and then she had to run, but by then Meg had reached me on my cell and we arranged...."

Charlie Ravioli is plenty familiar to all of us. I call my daughter and get her answering machine, so I try her cell. She'll get back to me. I go into my office and open my e-mail and find a message from her. "Where are you?" she wants to know. "Your phone's been busy all day." My children send me e-mails to tell me what time they're going to call me because we have something to discuss. Instant messages pop up on my computer when I'm in the middle of a note to somebody else. "Hi! How are you? This is Gail." Like Charlie Ravioli, I don't always answer because I have to run.

Everybody is way busy. People in my family tell me, "Slow down! Take it easy!" I have meetings and writing projects to send off to my editors and a fund-raising party to co-host and artwork to take to a show and a reception for an artist and family coming in for the weekend and the phone is ringing and I don't have time to read all my e-mails and everybody I know is in the same fix.

It used to be different. Really. Adam Gopnik contrasts our wildly busy modern world with that of Benjamin Franklin, who "boasts of his industriousness" but "never complains about being too busy, and always has time to publish a newspaper or come up with a maxim or swim the ocean or invent the lightning rod." Not to mention charming all the ladies in the French court. But you don't have to go back to the 1700s to find a more placid world.

Getting out of my littered car I look over my shoulder and promise to make time before my appointment the next day to stop by the car wash. My father used to telephone the real people at his garage and someone brought him a clean new car to drive while they took his car to the shop, checked everything, washed and polished it inside and out and delivered it. Then they thanked him for his business.

The dry cleaning and laundry truck called regularly at our house. The drivers took away our dirty things and brought them back clean with all the linens starched and ironed. The bakery truck arrived a couple of times a week with fresh bread and rolls. Our milkman rattled bottles outside our windows every morning and by the time we were ready for breakfast our fresh milk and cream and butter and eggs were standing outside the back door inside the insulated container the company provided. When my mother ran out of groceries she telephoned her order to the store for delivery, then sat down and wrote charming notes to her friends. There was plenty of time for real people before Charlie Ravioli came to town.

Today, we take the shards of our day to the dry cleaner, run a few loads of clothes through the washer and dryer, fold them and put them away (nobody has time to iron anymore), aware while we're working that we're stealing minutes from something else we ought to be doing. Our multiple trips to the grocery store and the local library become social occasions where we talk too long to the real people behind the checkout counters because we're tired of talking to cyborgs.

Olivia has her small fingers on the pulse of America. "How was your day?" Adam Gopnik and Martha asked each other. And when Olivia was three, they answered, "Oh, you know... just... bumping into Charlie Ravioli."

Not long ago I successfully completed a do-it-yourself checkout at a large discount store. At the airport in North Carolina our son entered data into an electronic panel and handed us our boarding passes. I encountered Olivia only a short time ago and already it's clear that in my life as in hers, Charlie Ravioli is alive and well in all the places where the real people used to be.

Bringing The Harvest Home

Chances are you aren't the person you think you are. Living is a voyage of discovery and when the harvest comes in, you could wake up and find yourself different, somehow, from the person you put to bed the night before.

The process of self discovery never ends. As teenagers we look back on our childhoods and say, "Well, that's over." But the child lives on inside us and may lead us along new and different paths. Our education isn't over when we finish school. We keep on learning as long as we live and assimilate new thoughts and bend to new concepts, taking tentative steps along broad avenues of exploration, even adventure.

Weather changes us – changes our moods, our energy levels, our choice of foods. The light salads and simple omelets that were so perfect a couple of months ago have lost their appeal. It's fall now, and I want big kettles of homemade soup, crackpots full of hearty stews, fresh-baked bread, sugar in my coffee.

At harvest time each year I am drawn to my stove, though I lack the talent to be a trendy, reliable cook. I never worked in a warm farmhouse kitchen, helping my mother produce tender fried chicken and succulent hot pies. My mother supervised the kitchen from a distance and in the kitchen itself our cook ruled with an iron hand. She had no time for children asking questions when the pots were simmering and the cake ready to come out of the oven. I have few kitchen memories, those few pleasant enough, but none of them designed to make a cook of me.

At our Sunday dining room table when I was a child, two meats, homemade breads, elaborate salads and our choice of desserts appeared as if by magic. We ate fresh shellfish from the ocean, eggs from the farmyard, vegetables and fruits from the legendary New Jersey truck farms that began just a few miles from our town. I grew up with an appreciation for fine food and not the least idea how to prepare it.

After my mother's death, my stepmother and her family showed me a side of food preparation that made me swear I'd never learn to cook. On holiday occasions her large family visited. The men gathered in the living room and library to sip cool drinks and enjoy football games while the women rushed around the steamy kitchen, hair disheveled and faces flushed from heat and exertion. As I compared what the women did with what the men did, the choice appeared obvious: I learned everything I could about football.

During my college years I experimented with food, finding inexpensive meals at small ethnic cafes. While living in England, I made visits to the Continent where I relished spring asparagus in Belgium and *toast aux champignons.* In Parisian cafes there were pastries and coffees. In Holland I woke to steaming cups of mocha and haunted the docks where vendors offered smoked eel on toast. On hot summer mornings in Switzerland, I breakfasted in a lush outdoor landscape on gruyere cheese, homemade bread and fresh strawberry preserves. Yet among all these gustatory delights, the only thing I learned to prepare was a genuine English cucumber sandwich and a proper pot of tea.

Home again, I met the man I married – a man from a large North Dakota farm, grounded from birth in food production, preservation, preparation and appreciation. As a young engineer living in city digs with three fellow graduates, Dick did all the cooking. He liked it well enough, he told me, but most important, cooking meant he never had to do the dishes. Early in our courtship he escorted me to the kitchen in my apartment and taught me how to cook a perfect egg, over easy. Immediately after our wedding, he introduced me to his butcher.

Over 20 years of daily kitchen duty for a family of seven, I learned to cook well enough but it was more duty than art. In mid-century America, women with large families complained of "slinging hash" and liked to quote a popular author: Fix yourself a dry martini, she advised, and stare sullenly at the stove.

My aversion to cooking slips its leash when I step out on the porch in the early morning and there's a nip in the air. The kitchen is the most inviting place in the house when the days draw down early. My mind goes immediately to hot oatmeal, that everlasting classic our mothers told us would "stick to our ribs."

In the fall, I come close to capturing the joy of cooking and remind myself that voyages of self discovery don't require air fares. It doesn't take travel to expand life's horizons. Not one of us lives long enough to fully satisfy the questing of the human mind, to explore all the facets of our built-in databases. In fall I find myself relishing the relief from employment tensions my new lifestyle grants me, the time out to probe the worldwide web of good food and the timeless art of preparing it with respect. Our five basic food groups these cool days are garlic and fresh ginger, olive oil, fennel and white wine with a variety of supporting casts.

Philosopher and poet Maya Angelou writes, "Life is pure adventure, and the sooner we realize that, the quicker we will be able to treat life as art: to bring all our energies to each encounter…we can invent new scenarios as frequently as they are needed."

I am not the same person I was when summer laid its warm hands on my shoulders. I feel at home in my warm and steamy kitchen, with its hearty aromas and flavors whose richness counterweights cool gray days. Each change of season brings its own discoveries, opens our minds and dangles in front of us the promise of new identities. In my kitchen these days I blend and taste, exploring food as art, changing myself, and after my fashion, bringing the harvest home.

The Passages Of Time

The view in spring from the upper deck of our house is of cantilevered rooftops on neighboring houses, geometric shapes that slash through a scrambled sorcery of bare branches. Fifteen years ago the trees were shorter and the rooftops floated over them. Now the buds of new leaves lay spring patterns against a pale sky and in another month my deck will be curtained by leaf and branch, sight lines tunneled down and across but no longer up and out. The geometry of rooftops will disappear under a canopy of green and my apparent world will narrow, governed by the march of the seasons and the tangled relevance of time.

Time. We write of it, sing of it, build aphorisms around it. Time is money and sleep knits up our cares and by the time you get to Phoenix she'll be waiting. Memory strolls down the corridors of time and for most of us, a time recalled is a timeless scene, a stage set imprinted somewhere behind our eyelids. My parents harbored cameo visions of the cataclysm that was World War I. To my generation, with no memory to guide us, that war was only a story in the pages of dusty leather-bound volumes anchoring a bookshelf in the family library, detailing events for us of a time that wasn't there.

Twenty years passed between 1918 when The Great War ended and 1938, when the world began accelerating toward World War II. The war in Vietnam that began 40 years ago remains vivid to those who lived it. But there is no relevance between Saigon and Baghdad for the young men and women serving in the Middle East. Parallels collapse in the flow of generations. We don't learn from history because we haven't the tools to view the past in perspective.

Does it matter? The Western world looks to eternity, relating it to a future of timelessness, while in the East the focus of existence is the ever-present "now." A melancholy old song tells us a kiss is just a kiss, a sigh is still a sigh and fundamental things apply, as time goes by. Time, flowing seamlessly, in an unknown place while our minds are centered elsewhere.

Time flies, we say, creating images of a racing pigeon or a soaring rocket. We speak of the inseparable propriety of time as if it were a thing we could wrap our arms around and carry with us. Look into the seeds of time, the poets propose, but where are the sprouts of new plant life and what sort of fruit ripens from those seeds? "O World! O Life! O time!" the poets sing and we read the notes and hum the tune, trying to keep time to the music.

Scientists speak of time travel and in fact it's possible already to leave a destination and arrive, miles distant, earlier by the clock than the time we left. Conservative thinkers tell us to forget it, that it's nothing at all of any significance, merely a factor in the way time zones are defined. But maybe it's more than that, a droplet on the breaking wave of the time barrier, something akin to Wilbur and Orville's contribution to the sonic boom inherent in the fact of flight. Maybe our journeying against the clock represents a wrinkle in time, a pleat, a tiny fold, a small prophecy beyond our imagining, a precursor however distant of "Beam me up, Scotty." Oliver Sacks, writing in *The New Yorker* magazine, says "We have unlocked time, as in the seventeenth century we unlocked space, and now have at our disposal what are, in effect, temporal microscopes and temporal telescopes of prodigious power. With them we can...observe, contracted to a few minutes through computer simulation, the thirteen-billion year history of the universe from the big bang to the present.... " Creation exploration: a pastime that questions the existence of times past.

The passing of events through the fine mesh of generations is like the passing of the torch in governments. Little true memory carries over to guide or to serve. New absolutes take control, new ideas surface, and memories are transformed to other places, other rooms, like old photographs burnished by a harsher or more candescent light. Through all the silent reaches of time each generation lives in the spirit of its ethos because there's nowhere else to live and we have become very, very good at convincing ourselves that the worst of times are the best of times.

Time is an ever-rolling stream, as we know when we call to apologize for missing a meeting or, heaven forbid, a dinner. I knew it was scheduled for Wednesday, we say, but I didn't know it was the 16th, or I knew it was the 16th but didn't know the date fell on a Wednesday. We are not really comfortable with time which is by is nature tricky and deceitful. If we were we would have no need for the watches on our wrists and the clocks in our houses, on schoolroom walls, in air terminals and train depots and bus stations. We know when it's time for a little something, but our global village runs by Greenwich Mean Time, the thief and the avenger, that ever-circling hand of time, the deceptively soft and rhythmic tick we ignore at our peril.

In solemn tones we speak of a time to be born and a time to die, a time to reap and a time to mourn. We look for a time to come when our understanding will flower, when "time's printless torrent" will slow and show us its true course. Meanwhile, we pledge our allegiance to the end of time, forgetting that time knows no boundaries.

Generation after generation we struggle feebly in the gritty clutch of time. We don't yet get it, the ageless beauty of time, its mythic quality. We can't quite grasp it, can't get a hold on it, can't make it stop so we can take a long, close look at its gears and springs, its chips and circuits. It's springtime now and so our neighbors' rooftops recede behind a canopy of leaves as time, allied with place, stages a vignette to mark a season. Time itself doesn't march, it doesn't pass, it simply is, valid only in the now, seeping out of the seams of boxes we label yesterday, today and tomorrow. We go about the days of our lives relishing the saltiness of time, baffled by it, pondering the pithy terseness of the English pub master's final call as the establishment closes for the night, "Time, ladies and gentlemen. Time."

Jane Duncan Flink

The Relevance Of Final Gifts

The telephone call came Friday night. Dick's sister Esther, after a year-long battle with lymphoma, was leaving the hospital and going home to die. Early Saturday morning we pointed the car north on our way to the little town of Osnabrock, North Dakota, to spend these last precious days with Esther. As we drove we wondered what gifts we had to bring her. And what we would take away with us from this heart-wrenching experience.

Neither of us had ever sat at the bedside of a dying loved one. Like most people we celebrate the birth of a new baby, but death is not something we talk about. In a society all but drowning in a flood of eat-right, live-right, stay-fit programs, death is a non-subject. Most Americans seem to believe if you follow the right regimen you can forget about dying. Death is something that happens only to people less health-conscious than ourselves. We are a vigorous nation, confident that if we ignore it, death will go away.

But reality has a way of thrusting its nose under the tent-flap. Driving north on Interstate 29, we were painfully aware of our ignorance, less from the spiritual point of view (we know full well that to all things there is a season) than the practical: What do you say to a person who is dying? How do you help? What could we bring to Esther's bedside?

Earlier in the week of the telephone call, by mutual agreement among doctors and patient, Esther had decided to forego further treatment of her multiple cancers. And so her family took her home to her apartment in the town where she was born, where she raised her family, where she was the focal point of so much that was good. Two of her daughters, Kathy and Becky, came from their distant homes to take on all her nursing care. Family and friends gathered round for the last, long vigil.

Pastor Sandy Larson of Dovre Lutheran Church was a frequent visitor, serving all of us as spiritual advisor while dealing with her own grief as Esther's close friend. The day we arrived, she brought a small book to Esther's apartment, where I found it lying on a table. Called *Final Gifts,* the book was written by a pair of health practitioners with years of hospice experience.

Final Gifts explains in detail the physiological and psychological changes a dying person undergoes. Like birth, the book explains, dying can be hard work and the dying person needs the support, comfort and assurance of family and friends. The last senses dying persons lose are touch and hearing, so at the end they need comforting words and the laying on of hands, soothing hands, loving hands.

There was a bright window at the side of Esther's bed reflecting a relentless hot, dry summer day. A CD player on the windowsill filled the room with her favorite hymns. "How do you feel?" we asked her at first. "Not so good," she said, quietly, drifting in and out of drugged sleep, so unlike her lifelong strong and optimistic self that it broke our hearts.

Family members took turns sitting beside Esther's bed, holding her hand and talking softly to her. Taking our turn, Dick and I told her what the day was like, the kind of day she had lived for 80 years. "Gladys and Wilma made 32 kuchens this morning and Virgil thinks he has a buyer for the Missouri farm," we said. "We drove to Canada to buy June berries. Fred and Jeff are racing a storm to get the alfalfa crop in. Bob's canola fields are beautiful – bright yellow acres under a blue sky. You remember how that looks. Marilyn will be here soon; she's babysitting for the grandchildren. Bernice and Art are planning to move to an apartment – she will tell you more about that." We told her how much we loved her. We talked about how much we admired the way she had led her life.

One last time the girls lifted her into the wheelchair and rolled her out into the living room to be with family and friends gathered there, as we had gathered for family reunions over so many years. Suddenly, Esther became agitated. "Coffee!" she said, hoarsely. "Coffee!" Her daughters knew their mother, knew what she wanted. When you entered Esther's house she offered you a cup of coffee and fresh-baked treats, and terminal illness was no excuse for a breach of hospitality. Quickly, the girls made coffee, took little china plates from the corner cabinet, passed around handmade sweet bread brought by caring neighbors. Esther, content now, nodded off. Finally, her work was done.

We learned from *Final Gifts* that people often have trouble letting go because of deep-seated concerns or unresolved issues. When she couldn't speak anymore, we watched Esther's desperate fight to breathe, to live. Understanding her devotion to her children, Dick, eldest son in the family, said the words that would ease her mind. He told her that her children were all well and happy. That her family was all there together. That she had done her job and done it well. That everyone she cared about was praying for her. She had been a good and faithful servant and now her task was done It was time for her to start on the journey that would take her home to God.

Esther's breathing slowed and in time, peacefully, it stopped. Pastor Sandy called all of us to the bedside for a brief service in remembrance of Esther's baptism and we made a circle, hand gripping hand, and said the Lord's Prayer together. Then we found our way through our tears to the grassy verge outside the apartment building where dust hung in the hot, dry air, stirred up by grain trucks rattling by on their way to skyscraper elevators down by the railroad tracks.

Later that night, exhausted by grief, we sat in the quiet dark under a starlit sky on a porch at a family farmhouse on that vast high prairie. And it came to us that if the family's final gifts to Esther were our presence, our touch and our words, her final gift to us was of far greater value. She taught us that death isn't terrible. That dying is a passage from a place in time to a timeless place, and like all long and difficult journeys, it is a road best taken in the caring company of kindred souls.

Life Goes On

Life goes on. It sounds like an easy out, a callous maxim, an unfeeling dismissal. In reality, it is one of the most comforting elements of our world.

On Sept. 11, 2001, terror strikes New York and Washington in the form of airplanes used as bombs. Hurricanes lash through central Florida, New Orleans, Texas, gutting cities, shattering lives. Millions are dead in Darfur. Thousands of our troops and an untold number of civilians are dying in Iraq. To the stunned survivors it must seem that the future is closed for business. And yet even then, even now, life goes on.

After disaster, the imperative present rivets us. Even in desolation there is food to find, shelter to share, rebuilding to begin. In our privileged land, a bad tooth takes us to the dentist. There is that speech we promised to give in a nearby city. Wherever we have slept the sun rises in the morning and somewhere the laundry whirls its way through the washing machines.

As friends of ours wait for the doctors to give a green light for a bypass operation for the husband and father, life goes on. A daughter travels to be with her mother during the surgery, now put on hold until the patient is stable. A week later, the daughter's career calls and she catches a plane back home. Life goes on, in this case unfolding a happy ending.

I wondered as our family began the process of selling the *Boone County Journal* if there was life after journalism. I found soon enough that life goes on. In my home office I am at work on page design, editing and technical writing for a seven-county greenways project in the Kansas City area. In this retirement life we reacquaint ourselves with simple pleasures every day we spend apart from the grinding intensities of editorial positions, revenues and deadlines. Life goes on, even after journalism.

Life doesn't always go on the way we think it should, nor does it accept our guidance on its journey. When we came home, leaving the newsroom behind, I was shocked at the amount of neglect evident everywhere in our house. We were home again, but it didn't feel like home. We had paused here for refreshment, but we weren't really living here. Most of our energy and a huge amount of our time was directed elsewhere.

Lacking the time and the will to deal effectively with the stuff of everyday living, I had shoved it into drawers, closets, out of sight, in boxes under the bed. There was "stuff" everywhere, the shards of overscheduled lives familiar to thousands of double career-path families.

In April, I would have told you, "Give me a couple of months and this house will be shipshape." But it didn't work out that way. Writing assignments intervened. Volunteer commitments multiplied. A terminal illness in the family took us away from home. We opted out for a badly needed vacation. And life went on.

There is a small linen closet in the hallway between the public and private portions of our house, its shelves bulging with sheets for beds we sold years ago, threadbare towels, a lamp shade without a lamp and monogrammed linens that will never see an ironing board again. Inside the closet lives the spirit of a *feng shui* dragon who hisses at me as I pass the closed door. I need to roll up my sleeves and clear the closet, but the ongoingness of life keeps intervening. I'll get it done one of these days, I say over a fast-running stream of weeks.

The flow of weeks never falters, not even when a plant announces mass layoffs and job hunts begin. Even in disastrous times, a child brings home an unsatisfactory report card and parents meet with a teacher. A church meeting calls us out of a cocoon of sorrow. There is grass to mow, leaves to rake, snow to shovel.

Life goes on after the worst of tragedies, luring us out of deep grief and uncontrollable anger and pain. Best of all, life goes on even as we grieve, struggling to deal with loss. At funerals families come together, talk, remember the past, look to the future. We take on a new job, drive new roads to work and life goes on, pacing us as we adjust, layering bits of solid ground under our unstable feet.

"Get on with your life," is the message that comes through in times of recovery from blow after blow to our shared sense of what is normal, what is secure, what is good. Life going on is what we count on, whether or not we nurture its progress, the solid base that disciplines us and brings us comfort after tragedy and loss, even heartens us when small dragons hiss from closets where clutter silently multiplies.

Life goes on, with us or without us. We've heard it all our lives, words that seem cynical, thoughtless, uncaring. Words that in fact reflect the immutable reality of human existence, that teach us to respect the small daily tasks that sustain us. In its steady forward progress, life's on-going instructs us in endurance, overwhelms unbearable grief and sorrow and impels us toward a vision of the realities tomorrow holds in store.

Chapter Three: Beguiled by Place

Treasure In The Woods

"Our relationship with the places we know and meet up with...is a close bond, intricate in nature, and not abstract, not remote at all. It's enveloping, almost a continuum with all we are and think." ~ Tony Hiss, "The Experience of Place."

In 1976 we built a brick house on 33 acres at the crest of a hill above a small wild lake in northern Boone County. We called it The Clearing because that's what it was – a cleared space surrounded by woodland. Silver Fork Creek defined our western boundary and the pasture where our house was built still held hummock rows made by old plows before the shallow soil gave up its last meager goodness and the farmers moved on or died out and the forest began reclaiming the land.

An old-growth tree line separated our yard from a pasture that sloped down into the woods, into a wide marshy place where the creek spread out to form a small wetland. We used a stand of dead trees there for firewood and up at the house, the sound of sawing drifted distantly in and out of open windows. When the intertwining branches of the old trees were gone, letting sunshine stream in, a thicket of river birch sprang up like a small nursery.

About a mile east of us down a narrow gravel road was the derelict farmhouse that once ruled the acreage. There were no doors left on the house and we walked inside and up and down the stairs and looked at peeling strips of faded wallpaper and carved woodwork on the window frames and talked in hushed voices, thinking of the people who had lived there. In time we had a neighbor, a family who bought the acres where the farmhouse stood and built a new house and tried to salvage the old.

Our three girls had moved off to college, and we had three boys at home – two of our own, and a third son we acquired as an exchange student from Argentina. On weekends in early spring when the house was sleeping, I pulled on boots and tramped the woods. Along the creek side near the culvert under the gravel road I found a downed tree that formed a perfect bridge and walked out along it, looking down on a carpet of springing trout lilies. Farther inland, if you stood at the top of the ravine that dropped steeply into the creek you could see through the woods an island formed by the water's route, covered in a blue haze of flowers. When I climbed down for a closer look I found drifts of Virginia bluebells and after that, every spring, I went looking for them and they were always there.

To get to the birch thicket you crossed the lawn at the back of the house, passed through the oak and hickory tree line and followed the downhill slope of the pasture to the verge of the woods. I carried my camera one misty day to photograph light and water on the birches and rambling east, found a sea of May apples, rain dappled and looking for all the world like the umbrellas of Cherbourg. Just beyond I came upon a small black buggy in the woods, or the remains of a buggy, not a farm wagon as you might expect in a rural setting, but a fancy buggy that once had a small leather seat and a black fabric top, all rusting away, leaving an intricate chassis and tall wheels akilter on the forest floor.

The buggy was treasure, true treasure, in the middle of an ordinary wood and I wondered how it came to be there. Was it displaced by a Model T Ford that thrust its noisy nose into a farmer's long-gone barn, and like the old horses that pulled it, was put out to pasture? I walked around the stylish little buggy in the hush of the woods, full of wonder, aware of the same reverence we felt in the old farmhouse, the silent awe we bring to work done long ago by hands not our own, by those others who loved and hoped, strove and achieved, failed and despaired and then passed on, taking their mysteries with them.

We might have tried to retrieve the buggy, to carry it piecemeal up the hills but it seemed at home where it was and we left it there. We lived at The Clearing for 14 years and each spring I visited the buggy and each year there was less of it, the rounded wood of its wheels straightening awkwardly as the iron bindings rusted away.

Albums of photographs recall our brick house on the hill – Christmas and lawn parties, flower borders we planted, a line of teenage boys stocking the woodpile and views from every vantage. A photograph hanging on my wall captures the sense of inevitability that was strong that day when I found the buggy in the woods. Some things can't be caught by a camera's lens – the distant blue haze of the bluebells, the hummock rows left by old plows, the sleepy evening calls of the coyotes when we sat in our yard on fall evenings watching the moon rise over the trees.

Our time at The Clearing was brief, as we count time. We came there long after Indian hunting parties camped along the creek, well after farmers tilled the soil and someone left a buggy where a pasture met a wood. We left that place a few years before new houses sprang up across the road above the lake and closed around the brick house on the hill.

Did we leave behind artifacts of our own haunting, there for others to find as we found the marks of plows and the occasional arrowhead and the buggy in the woods? Do today's householders walk where we walked, look for bluebells in the spring and listen to the moonrise call of coyotes? And find themselves changed, as we were changed, by the presence of the past, compelling patterns fashioned by the whims of nature and human habitation sustained on the land.

Jane Duncan Flink

The Shape Of Home

Winston Churchill said we shape our buildings; then they shape us. Maybe that explains our family's ultimate agreement, after months of indecision, not to sell our house. Maybe this 20-year-old dwelling has shaped us in its image, molded us to its peculiarities, spoiled us with its views. Architect Wallace E. Cunningham says, "Above all else, a building must have a soul and communicate something that cannot be seen or felt in any other place." Our house is talking to us. "Stay here, why not?" it says.

So we are newly alert to our relationship with our dwelling and a captive audience for expert home designers. The magazine *Southern Accents* came last week and in bold red print declared, "Stave off winter's chill with some red hot color." It's a beautiful page with a red chair, lamp, fabrics and tableware, but who doesn't decorate with red in January? Left over from the holidays are red glasses, candles and flowers that don't shout "Christmas!" so you don't have to put them away. What a gift, to give them the imposing purpose of staving off winter chill!

The January issue of *Architectural Digest* arrived this week with its annual 100 best architects and designers commenting on the shape of our homes in the 21st century. Right out of the gate they take aim at excess. Marc Appleton of Santa Barbara declares the "McMansion syndrome" is waning and designer Paul Vincent Wiseman of San Francisco writes, "One perfect room is better than a monster house with cheapened details." Tom Kligerman stays on message: "No one is impressed today by acres of drywall. Of interest to us now is more concentrated work on a reduced canvas."

Which is good news for those of us with small canvases who believe with Tokyo architect Akira Watannabe that to become a home, a house must be a living environment for people.

I pore over all the stories about the chosen architects and designers but my mind harks back to staving off winter's chill, and I wonder about painting my home office terra cotta red. Designer Barbara Berry of Los Angeles would approve of my red room. She likes "...the idea of living for ourselves instead of for others, casually and elegantly, as the Europeans have always done." I don't know if terra cotta walls would be enough to make my office "casual and elegant." But if I paint my walls red, it will surely be to please myself.

The design experts talk about the burgeoning technologies that will affect the shape of our homes. New York designer David Easton says, "Next, and most critical, will come a study of how population, demographics and technology are changing the way we live and think and the way we design." Architect Graham Gund sees "... experimentation at many new levels...especially with green and sustainable materials."

Designer Mica Ertegun forecasts "... divisions of spaces to respond to today's way of living." Does this mean the demise of the classic three-bedroom, two bath ranch house? Mariette Himes Gomez envisions "... a renewed interest in a luxurious living room and less emphasis on the kitchen and bath...." Good news for those of us whose houses were built before kitchens required acres of pricey granite counters and bathrooms became shrines to the *haute monde* of ancient Rome. I'm afraid our "dated" facilities reflect a time when the ideal kitchen and bath required only adequate storage space, appliances and fixtures that worked, good lighting and surfaces that were easy to clean.

It surprised me that top designers and architects are so eager to shape our homes for comfort. Sore feet at the end of a rough day get as much attention as a choice example of chinoiserie. The Los Angeles firm of Hendrix/Allardyce uses scale and proportion "... to create a constant rhythm, yet one that gives you a calm, almost spiritual feeling." London's Kelly Hoppen seeks to create harmony and balance. Robert Kime of Marlborough, England, wants us to bring out all our fine things and put them to use, his definition of a life of ease. Marjorie Shushan of New York says tranquility and quiet luxury are essential. Karin Blake of Malibu is one of several designers who urge, "less of everything."

I'm paying attention to the experts because getting reacquainted with our house – viewing it as a family home again, not a place to crash after a long day in the newsroom, or a product on the market – puts our muscles and brains to work. These January days I have time to read the stacks of home design magazines and catalogs stacked next to every comfortable chair. Snow falls, the day's work is done, Murphy the cat settles in my lap, music plays softly in another room, tranquility reigns.

In deference to the spirit of design, I move a red glass vase to a west window where the winter sun in the full flood of a late afternoon strikes flares of hot color and sends them dancing over walls and ceiling like reflections of the hearth fires that warm us and welcome us home.

The Ins And Outs Of Downsizing

I scan the garage sales and country auctions in the newspaper with new eyes this year. We're doing very little collecting and a lot of downsizing and there's nothing better than the classifieds to remind you that you have way too much stuff.

We did some remodeling this year that meant removing the contents of two china cabinets and I realized, as I carted every piece of my collection of amber Sandwich glass to my office to get it out of the traffic, that I have more of it than I'll ever use. One of our daughters has started to collect the pattern and I can give her a service for four and never miss it. This comes of having the entire family – garage sale addicts all – scouting for amber glass from Minnesota to North Carolina. They're not finding much anymore because I have just about everything that was ever made and what I don't have is probably a blessing.

We're planning a visit to Jim and Jamie in Kansas City soon and Jamie was excited on the telephone. "I'm so glad you're coming this weekend," she said. "Riss Lake is having its community garage sale." I heard the news with something like apprehension, knowing when it comes to garage sales my self-control isn't everything it could be. The Riss Lake sale will certainly pose a threat to our downsizing.

Last time we were in Kansas City we were out on the hunt, looking through some old silver in a garage, when my eye traveled to a corner where I spied a rectangular walnut piano bench with a hinged top. We are downsizing, and I had no business looking at a piano bench but I had to ask how much the lady wanted. When she said $10 and it had belonged to her grandmother, Dick said, "Put it in the car." By the time we had the bench refinished we had invested considerably more, but standing at the foot of our four-poster bed it looks as if it belongs there, and every morning when I sit down to put on my shoes I wonder what I did without it.

When we began downsizing a year ago, we did what everybody does. We kept some things we should have sold and sold some things we should have kept. I sold all of my screen porch furniture and the camelback sofa from the family room and a small china cabinet, and I wish I hadn't, though this gives me some legitimate space to fill.

When the sun is shining on a Friday or Saturday morning, and the temperatures are comfortable, and we have no major projects on the schedule, Dick will look at me and say, "How about it – shall we look in on a couple of garage sales?" In the car we say to each other, "Now, don't let me buy anything really stupid."

This week, at the first stop I pick up a very small brand new roaster pan because the one I have is showing wear, and Dick says to me, "Is that stupid or not?" And I say definitely not.

As much as I love going to garage sales, I'd rather be stung by scorpions than stage one of my own. Everybody I know who has a garage sale tells me they made a couple of hundred dollars but I believe the most I ever brought in was something like $53.10. Given the effort it takes to amass hundreds of items, tag them, display them and sit in the garage all day, it just isn't worth it. My family tells me I'm too Scotch to run a good garage sale. I won't part with any of the really good stuff.

Chuck's wife Marjorie is as enthusiastic about garage sales as anyone I know. Marjorie and I decided long ago that garage sales are like deer season – it's the hunt more than the harvest that puts fire in our eyes. Marjorie solved the problem every garage saler faces – picking up too many goodies and winding up with too much stuff. She made an arrangement with an antique store in town to take her valuables on consignment. As a result she can hunt to her heart's content, and anything she can't use goes to the shop. In the long run, she says, she has a lot of fun and even makes a little pocket change.

It's amazing the things you learn from a major effort to downsize. First, you learn that all the things you've been saving for the children aren't the things your children would be caught dead with in their new houses. Items that were so chic on the well-dressed dinner table of the 1960s, like small crystal salt cellars with tiny silver spoons, and water goblets with curvy stems and big bowls, may be popular again in about 50 years but right now they aren't worth the tissue paper it takes to wrap them. And nobody younger than 60 wants anything to do with polishing a lot of silver or ironing Irish linen damask tablecloths and napkins.

Downsizing teaches us to cherish things we keep because we love them and discard things we keep because somebody special gave them to us or because they belonged to somebody in our family. When you fill a rental cubicle with household items and six months later can't remember what's there without looking at the list, it's time to get serious about weeding out your worldly goods.

This spring we have a few plastic bins stacked in the large storage room, one shelf unit of collectibles in the small storage room and we don't want to talk about the garage. It's time to tackle these last projects because we are downsizing, and we've put a lot of work into it, and this is no time to buy – or keep – anything stupid.

Color Me Glad

We live and dream in a Technicolor world. Color has meaning for us, when we think about it, bends our moods, stimulates our senses, and overwhelms our emotions. If I were a child I would paint summer red and yellow and seashore-sand with drifts of white blossoms under high blue skies. The coolness of autumn balances earthy reds against sienna, blends mossy greens with gold and brown, all hazed by a gauzy veil of wood smoke in the air.

When I think of winter I remember the lavender dawns years ago in our big white house on a hill in Wisconsin. On a below-zero morning the children bundled up for school in the warm kitchen and our three riding horses, their coarse winter coats insulating them against a world of knee-deep snow, waded to the kitchen door looking for treats. When the sun had yet to show its face, the pale lavender air tinted snowdrifts the color of the summer lilacs that lined our lane.

Spring in central Missouri was deep pink when we first came to live among the limestone bluffs above the lake. Redbud trees were everywhere, layering against the screens of the porch and draping branches heavy with bloom over two storeys of decks. The air itself seemed tinted rose, redolent of every remembered scent of spring.

Fifteen years later the wild redbuds, trashy, short-lived trees for all their breathtaking beauty, stand sparsely in our woods. On the screen porch on a late spring afternoon, I set a glass of iced tea on a side table, settle into a wicker rocker and open a book. But a strong, hot wind blows off the lake, lashing the branches of frail redbuds against the sturdy white trunks of tall sycamores and cottonwoods, drawing my attention away from the ordered black and white of the written word.

Of course spring, the season of fertility, is more than pink air. Spring is a preview of coming attractions, a contrast of dark brown earth and golden daffodils, of vivid red tulips with black exclamation points in their hearts. Virginia bluebells drift down garden slopes, neighboring the ferny foliage of the bleeding heart. In every springtime, somewhere there are lilacs, their blossoms and scent so entwined in our consciousness that they blur our very senses.

There is a wonderful old song about a failed love affair based on the many themes of color. The song is called "Color Me Blue," and the poignant line, "Color me – lonely now," is accented by a break in rhythm and melody, just as the colors we live with affect our moods and break the rhythms of our lives.

Some years ago there was a board game that explained the psychology of color, or so it claimed. Players chose color cards and their choices were analyzed in pseudo-scientific terms. There was something about "casting out greens," but the point was that color defines us when we are aware of it and even when we are not. Color us chameleon, the game seemed to say.

A friend in Florida writes that she is painting the walls in her house pure white, surrounding herself with the bright promise of primary color against a snowy background. I cannot imagine the casual wealth of color in a Florida cycle of seasons where vivid bromeliads flourish under the dining room window and householders in February pluck fat, golden lemons from a courtyard tree. Use all your crayons to color Florida in its throbbing tropical heat.

In our house I like backgrounds to mute their presence. Two years ago we painted three rooms celadon green, casting out a too-warm peachy-beige that made the walls seem to lean inward. The cool greens lived up to our expectations, bringing measurable calm to our over-scheduled lives, coloring us easier and more serene.

Each of us lives in a world defined by color, our seasons accented by the lavender of a winter morning, the gentle haze of a fall day, the rosy glow of springtime.

In our April woods the trees are in bud now, promising a leafy canopy that will spread until it dominates the landscape, tinting the lake a brassy verdigris along the shoreline. In the intensity of deep summer heat it will be a little cooler here, where the foliage of towering trees filters the light and shades the air sunglass-green. Color me glad.

Spring In Missouri

When the wind blows warm from the west and the moon is full and there's moisture in the air; when the wild roses spring into bloom and a light amount of weeding and planting dampens the hair at the nape of your neck, you know it's springtime in Missouri.

Swinburne wrote, "When the hounds of spring are on winter's traces/ The mother of months in meadow or plain/ Fills the shadows and windy places/ With lisp of leaves and ripple of rain…With a noise of wind and many rivers…Blossom by blossom, the spring begins."

On a dewy dawn in spring in the Missouri River valley, young timber rattlers stir in the rocky outcroppings along the bluffs and succulent morels push up through blankets of leaves on the lee side of fallen oaks under the windblown snowflakes of late dogwood blossoms. Spring in southern Boone County drowns the senses. And it can scare you to death.

Earlier this year, sometime in March, the weather forecasters predicted a "long, cool wet spring." Long and cool is likely to balance out in a moderately less hellish August – an August with, perhaps, fewer bugs, lower temperatures and even a modicum of desperately needed rainfall. It's the "wet spring" that sends chills up our backs. If you lived through the Great Flood of 1993 you remember that a wet spring was about all we expected as we drifted into a natural disaster so devastating it carried a hundred-year designation.

Great floods deliver a misery all their own. When disaster strikes – fire, storm, tornado, hurricane – there's advance warning and you move your loved ones and cherished belongings to high ground or low cover and wait it out. When the destruction phase is over, as best you can you begin to rebuild your life.

But water is the very devil, and the Great Flood of 1993 was savage in the three-month torture it inflicted on the residents of Missouri's river cities. After September, when the worst of it was over, we looked back on the wet spring and those early July days when reports of serious flooding began to filter in to the *Boone County Journal*. We wished there had been big white letters in the sky: "Prepare for the Flood of the Century." Instead, our professional coverage lagged as we worked the story day by day. Before it was over, we'd seen heartbreak to last a lifetime.

If you stand on the bank of the Missouri River on an ordinary day, you look across a wide expanse of gray water with a deep, rapid current. But when the sun shines and shoreline trees dip branches in an easy breeze, the river is deceptively peaceful. Old timers know better. In 1993, after the July flood, the water receded from doorsteps in the little town of Hartsburg and the population of 130 people began to pull their lives together. There was a run on Lysol and Clorox at the local grocery. At the newspaper office one morning I stopped outside to talk to a wise old man through the window of his pickup truck. "It's too soon to be cleaning up," he said and I asked him why. "Because that old river always rises three times," he said. "You'll see."

As journalists we were accustomed to "spring rises" in Hartsburg, our nearest river city. In the fall of 1986 our newspaper covered a modest flood with a front-page photo of local farmers taking to their fields in jon boats.

Four years later, the *Journal* carried a story that began, "If it weren't for Perche Creek…things might not have been so bad when the Missouri River rolled over its banks May 17, 1990. But the sinewy Perche, which snakes its way into Boone County at the Randolph County line and empties into the Big Muddy at Easley, passes through the middle of

McBaine. And last week, the Perche poured a burden of runoff water into the little community, backfilling areas that rain and the Missouri River had only begun to dampen."

We know the spring rise of the river and its tributary creeks is a force to be reckoned with, but in 1993, lacking that message in the sky, it took too long for our newsroom, securely high and dry, to catch the tide of a disaster of monumental proportions.

Prior to 1993, the flood year of record was 1951 when the Missouri River crested over 34 feet at Hartsburg. In early July of 1993, the river rose six feet in 10 days. The levee broke at Hartsburg and farms and homes in the fertile bottomland went under water, washing away a year's income for local farmers. Rain in Missouri, Kansas, Nebraska and Iowa fell without ceasing. The second rise came a few weeks after the first. The third rise in early fall set records; an eight-foot wall of sandbags stretched across Hartsburg's main street, a fragile barrier between the townspeople and restless currents that filled the vast river valley from bluff to bluff.

Each spring in the great fertile bottomland of the Missouri River we wait for news of runoff from the high plains in the far north and watch the skies, not for announcements, but for fat clouds heavy with rain. Spring in Missouri is a time of beauty and drama and apprehension. This year a moderate early river rise caught our attention but the waters went calm, and the long, cool spring taught us only that "the meaning of May was clear," as sweet weather soothed our senses with the blessing of normalcy.

At our steeply-pitched homestead on Lake Champetra heavy spring rain enters a sluiceway above the road, follows a conduit under it and roars down the easternmost border of our land, rushing over a spillage of boulders, undermining trees and surging in long brown fingers into the lake. An overflow valve releases excess lake water into the wilds of Cedar Creek, which carries it to the Missouri. Friends and family love to visit in the springtime to experience from a top floor screen porch the sight and roar of the tumbling waters.

But if you know spring in these river hills, even as you are charmed by wild rains and prairie roses tumbling down banks to the lakeshore, you are aware of the timber rattlers coiled in the warm dry places in the deep woods, and you keep in mind how the earth shakes underfoot when the wide Missouri thunders at floodtide. And you realize that no one but a great poet could do justice to the drama of this Missouri, when the land wakens after a long winter and the dogwood swirls white snowflakes through new-green woods and the rivers rage in the springtime.

A Monument To Broken Dreams

On a sunny Thanksgiving afternoon the trees are bare at Ha Ha Tonka State Park in central Missouri, and the picnic benches deserted. Family groups like ours are walking off turkey dinners along the broad paved trails leading to the ruins of the Snyder mansion, a castle built in the forest on a pinnacle above a rock-strewn gorge and with it, a carriage house that once sheltered 100 horses and 30 automobiles. In 1976 vandals wrote the final fiery finish to this testament to wealth and innovation when they set fire to the stone tower that housed servant's quarters and the water tank that had supplied the house.

This is a ghostly place, a monument to broken dreams. Wind rustles among the ruins like the echo of a waltz drifting over the castle's moonlit terrace in a social season long ago. The stone terrace fronts the brink of a limestone bluff. Over the stone balustrade you look straight down, far down to a finger of the Lake of the Ozarks winking deep blue, fringed with tiny houses and miniature boat docks.

Only the walls of the castle and the terracing remain and when you walk up the broad stairs you feel you might keep on walking through a towering front door into the warmth of a great hall, an atrium rising three and a half stories to a window on the sky. Opposite the doorway three Moorish arches once reflected the Belle Epoque's delight in all things Arabesque.

The castle and its outbuildings, the trails and the setting were the dream of Robert McClure Snyder, born in Indiana in 1852. By 1870 Snyder's grocery business prospered in St. Louis and in 1880 he moved to Kansas City where he made his fortune in real estate, banking, oil and utilities.

Robert Snyder left his footprint on the structures at the park and his spirit wanders there, not unusual in the haunted hills of the Missouri Ozarks. When they met, one man and one 5,000-acre tract of Ozark wilderness bonded instantly and always. Snyder's vision matched his wealth and at the castle site today's visitors experience a touch of *frisson*, that grand French word that alone describes the combination of thrill and fear children seek telling spooky stories around a campfire.

"Here I will spend my leisure," Snyder wrote, "secure from the worries of business and the excitement of city life. I will fish and loaf and explore the caves of these hills, with no fear of intrusion." Yet in 1906, within a year of breaking ground for his dream castle, Snyder was killed in one of Missouri's first automobile accidents.

His obituary in the *Kansas City Journal* said he was a man who "understood big things and made them win by keeping up the fight when other men might have been ready to give it up." He was known for his ethics, his idealism and his dedication to his family. He wrote his son, "Lay down for yourself principles of truth – of honor – of self respect – and of unselfishness – and do not violate them – thus will your life be a success and a pleasure to you and every one who knows or meets you."

Altogether, Robert Snyder had four sons and it was they who made his dream a reality, completing the castle in 1922 much as their father had envisioned it. Did they manage, along the way, to fish and loaf and explore caves? Were there the kind of parties Edith Wharton writes about, the great dining hall sparkling with candlelight and porcelain and silver and six courses served? Or were there Gatsby bashes with bathtub gin and flappers in shockingly short chiffon dresses dancing antic Charlestons on the terrace while moonlight splashed on the stiff white shirtfronts of gilded youth and lit the bright hair of silk-stocking beauties?

The castle had its day, its very brief day and then it was leased as a hotel and in the 1940s, in the isolated splendor of those enchanted woods, fire broke out and everything that could burn in the house and stables was consumed – the great front door, the Moorish arches, the floors between storeys – leaving stone walls standing stark, the outline of a dream as insubstantial as the sand castles children build at the seashore. At Ha Ha Tonka there remains only the suggestion of a castle: stone walls open to the sky and the wide-ranging imagination of park visitors.

The park is more than the castle. Native Americans of the Niangua families settled there and Daniel and Nathan Boone and Zebulon Pike left relics of their passing. There is a natural bridge, a mammoth sinkhole, a gushing spring. Near a whispering dell are the caves we hope Robert Snyder found leisure to explore before his untimely death.

Bluffs tower 250 feet high and on one of them are the ruins of Snyder's castle where the carriage drive still sweeps under a porte-cochere built to shelter guests dismounting for the balls with the waltzes, the ones I was telling you about, where the music floats over the terrace. Have I missed a beat? I place one hand on a gentleman's arm, lower my eyelids and say demurely, yes, I would love to dance. Or was it only the whisper of the wind through a harmony of stone arches? All that's left of somebody else's Ozark dream.

Why We Live Here

I open the door to the porch with one hand and pick up the phone with the other. It's my doctor, reporting that a routine test is normal. "Get outside on this beautiful spring day," he prescribes. "Days like this – that's why we live here."

The phrase echoed as I shook out rugs and blankets and hung them over railings and chair backs for a dose of sunshine. Spring is a time for sweeping up and clearing out. Areas of the house that seemed cozy when window glass was cold to the touch and snowflakes sifted through the trees seem drab now, old and used and in need of refreshing.

Dick cut a daffodil that opened rapidly in the warm house, and I ate my lunch staring into the heart of its golden trumpet. In central Missouri we live optimistically ahead of ourselves, anticipating in winter these first spring days, in spring the hot twilight of a Fourth of July, in August the crisp bronze of an October afternoon and even as we are touched by autumn's glory, our thoughts mush forward into the purity of the first snowfall.

The intense variety of all these days came to mind when I vacationed with friends in Arizona in October. The first three days were glorious, each sunny morning exactly like the one before. By the fourth day, I had begun to scan the skies in search of a thunderhead, maybe, sweeping over the breathtaking panarama of a distant mountain range; to wish for a breeze to ruffle the pages of the newspaper I was reading on the covered patio. It is absolutely wonderful to live where there is constant sunshine, my friend told me. To know you can leave the cushions on the yard furniture and they won't be drenched by a sudden storm during the night. Ridiculously, an old TV commercial popped into my head. "Yes," I thought restlessly. "But where's the beef?"

In Missouri we are a week away from the first day of spring and there's plenty of "beef" coming before the last danger of frost is past in early May. Cooler weather is forecast in the next couple of days with rain, even a bit of snow. But in America's heartland, constant change is the norm, is what we expect. We know our seasons. Weather may be capricious, but we can see spring in the way the light casts shadows, hear it in the resurgence of bird calls in our woods, feel it as a warmer sun bronzes our faces.

In winter, going out can be an adventure and it can be hazardous. To be inside is to be safe and warm. But on the first warm day, when I open front and back doors to let clean air brush through the house, my heart lifts and I feel paroled. As free as our cat, Murphy, who crosses and recrosses the thresholds of the open doors, just because he can.

On our deck, the lettuce and spinach Dick plants in large pots are showing small green shoots. Just steps away from the kitchen, they'll make fresh garden salads before April is gone. Around our 80-acre lake, boats are coming out from under tarps, being trucked in from storage. When the water warms the fishermen will be out, calling to each other as they pass, telling the same tall tale – their wives sent them out to catch dinner.

This morning I shepherded a Carolina wren out the door of the screen porch and watched her fly away. An old friend, that wren – in other springs she has visited the living room, inspected Dick's closet, and nested in the wreath on our front door, making it off limits to human traffic until the eggs hatched and the fledglings took flight.

The return of the wren, the new shape of shadow, the warmth of the sun, the clean flow of air, the freedom from reclusion, the hearts of daffodils, the promise of fresh greens – all call for celebration as winter turns to spring. But I suspect we are as thrilled by change as much as anything else, by the way our lives shift in harmony with Missouri's four distinct seasons. Days like all of these – that's why we live here.

A Garage Of My Own

The designers on House and Garden TV are redecorating somebody's garage. They are painting the walls lime green and laying down bright blue snap-together tiles on the garage floor. I realize that my mouth is partly open, so I snap it shut.

I think about my own garage, only a few steps away outside the door to the back hall. You open that door at your peril, never knowing what might be on the other side. A baby raccoon died in there when he got caught in the garage door mechanism. It wasn't pretty. Our dog, Bandit, tried to chew his way through the door to the house when we closed him up in the garage one night long ago. The door has been repaired, but not exactly restored. There are brown recluse spiders in our garage. I've never seen one, but that's the nature of the brown recluse spider.

We have a late 20th century house so of course our garage is the first thing you see when you visit us. Whenever people are coming we call to each other, "Did you shut the garage door?" Not that the garage door is a thing of beauty, but it's a gift to guests compared to what's inside the garage.

I cannot fathom why 21st century Americans build their houses behind their garages. The garage is a latter-day stable, after all, and stables belong as far away from the front door as your property allows. A builder told me everybody wants a concrete driveway and concrete is too expensive for long driveways. An architect told me people like to show off their cars. But what do cars have to do with the garage? Are there people who actually have room in the garage for their cars?

At our house we talk a lot about organizing the garage. It goes on lists where everything else gets scratched off and then "clean the garage" appears at the top of the next list. If we ever redecorate our garage I will paint it spider-brown. The contractor who built this house used an optimistic off-white paint on four expanses of doomed drywall. What we need is wrinkled dried leaf spider-brown paint and the construction joists showing. Maybe old paint brush, dusty shelf, wrinkled dried leaf spider-brown paint. Or better yet, no paint at all.

In the designer garage the snap-together tiles on the floor have holes in them so water can drain away, the glamorous young hostess tells us.. Away where? I know where water goes in garages. It goes into the corners where it is wicked up by the doomed drywall. Have you ever known water to drain in a smooth stream out the garage door and into the drainpipe you put there to catch it?

In spite of trying to save face by keeping our garage door closed, sometimes we leave it open and storms blow rain into the garage. Dead leaves actually seek out garages. They whirl around in circles, looking for a garage to blow into. Engine oil falls on garage floors and peat moss and potting soil and turpentine and spray paint and car wax and window-washer fluid. Little birds make nests on stacks of storage bins. I'd hate to see those pretty blue tiles after about six months in your average American garage.

The television designers are installing matching cabinets. Shiny black matching cabinets with bright brushed chrome knobs, one with a place for hand tools, one with a pull-out counter for small electric saws and routers. There is a bright chrome bar for hanging garden rakes and shovels, tools you could pick up without getting your hands dirty, but there is a stainless steel sink just in case.

I think the designers are "funning" us, as the old folks used to say. I grew up in an old New Jersey town, so old you could trace where George Washington's troops marched. The town is made up of big old houses with big old trees out front and long driveways leading to small former barns out back, or a carriage house, or even a modern garage. You don't get to the front door by walking past the garage, you get to the front door by walking up a few steps to a big wrap-around porch with flower boxes on it.

My family had a carriage house out back. We called it "the barn" and one day I was playing with friends in an orchard next to the barn when we noticed a window on the second floor that we had never seen from the inside. We knew the blueprint well. On the ground floor there were two big horse stalls at the back (now empty), and room in front for the carriages (where we parked our cars), and a stairway going up the side wall to the groom's quarters (used for storage). There was no window showing indoors upstairs on that side of the building.

There isn't a kid in the world who could ignore a discovery like that, so we started rooting around and pretty soon we found one of the walls on the second floor didn't quite meet the floor. If you lifted up a board you could roll down into a shallow place and come up on the other side in a small room with the window. You talk about excited—we could hardly talk. We were sure our house had been a stop on the underground railway and poor fugitive slave persons had stayed there on their way to New England.

All this happened a long time after General Grant refused to accept General Lee's sword, but not long enough before people started building their garages next to their front doors.

I wish I had a big dark stable-like place with plain wood spider-brown walls out back where rain and leaves could blow in and it wouldn't matter. A place with room for our cars and enough left over to keep all our stacked storage bins and garden tools and paint and car wax close at hand. You don't need expensive cabinets in a garage like that. You can park the Porsche out front if you want to show off your car. Everybody ought to forget about designers and build their garages in the back yard where they belong.

Waiting For The Rain

There's a stillness in these late summer days, a breathlessness as if all the air has been suctioned out of every sunny afternoon. Everything waits for rain. We watch the Weather Channel on television. The storms pass above us, below us, west of us, east of us, missing us. Bodies tense, we lean in closer to the TV weather map, hoping.

Established shrubs in our gardens grow tipsy with wilt, their leaves hang listless, curling and crisp with drought. Trees droop. The giant hydrangea, that water-lover that boldly waved globes of white blossoms in July, lies squandered on the ground, its flowers draggled among dry leaves as if flattened by a rock hurled from the deserts of the moon.

The Missouri River at Jefferson City and Hartsburg tallies record low water stages and the unruffled surface of our own lake is rimmed by rusty banks. Shamelessly naked under a relentless sun, they're waiting for the lake-filling rains to come. Waiting.

In small towns nearby, shopkeepers doze through the end of summer. You could roll a bowling ball down main streets without hitting even an errant pickup truck bound to market for a roll of twine. Early summer's euphoria, kids larking on bikes, leaping into sparkling swimming pools, thronging leafy parks – all that is gone. Summer is boring now. Children yawn as another school year draws near, perk up over small pleasures – new packs, new pencils, new paraphernalia etched with celebrated logos. Forgetting how droning school will become, how they'll yearn for vacation time. Wal-Mart stocks shelves with Halloween costumes, ghostly apparitions, shivery, slithery autumnal things, while above the parking lot outside bits of high vapor drift by disguised as clouds.

At night sometimes sudden thunder cracks over our house and we look up from our books and Murphy the cat slides in behind my feet and peers out between my ankles. We hold our breath and wait, counting – the boom of thunder, a flash of lightning – how long in between? How close is the storm? The next boom is distant, the next crack only a bright flicker of heat lightning in a black sky. The cat ventures out, stretches himself and curls up like a dark fur rug against a light carpet, snoring gently.

The next morning is glaring and hot. The boys at the car shop, working in 100 degree heat, changing the oil in car after car, say it's blazing enough to start a fire in the oil pits. But it's always been like this in the Heartland. Pioneer Josiah Gregg learned about blazes when he set out from New Franklin, Missouri in 1848 headed southwest on the Santa Fe trail where heat lightning set vast prairies on fire.

"The perils (of) prairie conflagrations…when the grass is tall and dry… (can be) sufficient to daunt the stoutest heart," he wrote. A century later, Marc Simmons, writing for the *National Geographic* magazine remembers, "One August afternoon I had a firsthand view of the frightening power of a prairie fire. Topping a hill in my car, I caught sight of a dense cloud of smoke billowing along a three-mile strip of horizon. As I approached, the air grew hot and acrid…It was hard not to imagine the dread felt by early wagoners who, like Gregg, were pursued by one of these ravenous infernos."

Hot and acrid we understand, all right, in our own mock inferno, waiting for the rain. We stand in the narrow clearing of road that snakes around our lake and think of the dry kindling that floors surrounding acres of woodland. The skies over the lake are steel, blank, infinite. All around us dry leaves rustle, crying for water.

We are weary of this stillness, irritable and restless and cranky. Only the rain will bring relief and when it comes we'll want to run outside and lift our faces to the sky and feel the water drum against our eyelids.

Summer is almost over now. Looking up into a milky sky we see turkey vultures riding the air currents in widening spirals above the naked trees, sooty images against a blank canvas. We shade our eyes and watch them circle, watch them rock on fitful gusts, watch them watching us, waiting for the rain.

Lights Out

The lights went out just at dusk. Dick was on the phone talking to his brother in the hospital in Joplin and I had just picked up the latest issue of *The Atlantic* magazine when the power failed. Outside, the sky was a dirty white but vegetation at ground level was disappearing fast in the deepening twilight and in the house the walls, furniture and doorways were fading to black. At the end of a 90-degree day, an ominous silence replaced the comforting hum of the air conditioner.

Power outages are not a novel experience in southern Boone County and we've learned to cope. I stash flashlights and keep a few kerosene lamps in tiptop condition with fresh oil, clean chimneys and trimmed wicks. Pretty soon a lamp was glowing in the kitchen and another one ready to carry off to bed.

Jane Duncan Flink

What can you do when the lights go out? You can't read or work a crossword puzzle or refigure your budget or run a little laundry through or listen to the radio or watch television or warm up a snack. "Somebody needs to invent something to do when the lights go out," I said to Dick. "Somebody already has," he said. "It's called sleep. I'm going to bed. G'night dear." Dick sleeps well and loves his sleep so he trudged off down the hall happily enough, looking with his oil lamp like an illustration from "The Night Before Christmas."

We've all heard that Abraham Lincoln studied his law books at night by the light of a lantern, so I pulled a barstool up close to the oil lamp on the long counter in the kitchen and opened my magazine. It didn't take long to conclude that either people in Lincoln's day had eyes much keener than our own, or the story is nothing more than a charming fable.

Dick, whose childhood on the farm came before rural electrification, is comfortable in the dark. Often I come upon him sitting alone watching television in a dark room, and the first thing I do is hit the light switch. I think I'm doing him a favor. He usually lets me know that I'm not.

I love the light, all kinds of light from the white-hot noontime sun on bare beaches to the throbbing neon scald of an evening in Times Square in New York City. My dad took an electrical engineering degree from Auburn around 1915, a bold choice when electricity was in its infancy. He was fascinated by light and our house was brilliantly equipped and never totally dark.

It was a big house to begin with and after dark it blazed like the Titanic on the midnight Atlantic. We had lamps that threw light toward the ceiling for general conversation, special lights to cook by, shave by, sew by, read by. There was no nonsense about candles on the dining room table. Glass, crystal and silver sparkled under a chandelier carrying maximum wattage on multiple arms. I was careful not to let Dad catch me reading without a proper light directed at the page. When I was in high school, boys who had plans for a romantic end to a date fled like startled deer. Walking across our dazzling front porch was like taking the stage at the Hollywood Bowl.

I learned at my daddy's knee to keep night lights burning throughout in the house – near the kitchen sink, close to doors, in the bathrooms and hallways. I actually enjoy shopping for light bulbs and can dawdle away time picking and choosing among the shapes and sizes and wattages.

Preoccupation with light is as good a hobby as any, I guess. but what do you do when the lights go out and you're the only person awake in the house? Dick finds the dark warm and enveloping. I find it threatening and confusing, like a scuba diver who loses track of which way is up and which is down.

When the lights go out I remember the bedtime stories my mother used to tell me about God making the dark so the birds could doze off and the good little children could get their rest and wake up to a new day. But I was never really happy when the lights went out then, and I'm not crazy about it now.

"There is nothing there in the dark that isn't there in the daylight," my mother used to tell me to cure my fear of the night. You can't argue with the logic of that, even when you bark your shins on the chair you can see in the daylight but not in the dark.

So when the lights went out the other day I thought about the birds tucking their heads under their wings and I put away *The Atlantic* magazine and picked up my oil lamp. My shadow threw odd shapes on the walls before me and unseen things in the quiet black house nipped at my heels as I resolutely trundled off to bed.

Chapter Four: Wandering Woman

WHEN I AM OLD

When I am old I will wear a dusty blue silk crepe dress," I thought. It was my 10th birthday. I believed when I was old everybody would fly to work wearing aeronautic backpacks, that scientists would wear heavy iron shoes when they explored Mars because Mars doesn't have much gravity. While all this activity was going on, I could picture myself in my blue crepe dress. My hair would be silver white, pulled back into a bun at the nape of my neck. I would sit in an upholstered chair and my grandchildren would play around my feet. It made me happy, seeing myself like that.

But life changes us. Now I think when I am old, maybe I will live on a sea marsh in New England like Katherine Hepburn. I will wear comfortable men's trousers the way Kate always did with a bright men's tie cinching them around the waist and heavy knit sweaters with cowl necks to keep the wind out and my throat warm. I will paddle my own canoe on the marshes and in the Atlantic coves, stack the art I love on windowsills and let all the books I want to read pile up around my favorite chair. I'll never worry about dusting anything. Dick won't care and why else would it matter, when I am old?

My conscience intrudes on my dreams.

"Why Hepburn?" my conscience asks.
Why not Hepburn? I can match her, cheekbone for cheekbone.
"Try matching the hipbones," says my conscience in an impertinent tone of voice.

Maybe instead, when I am old, I will never really settle down. Dick and I will sell everything we own except a couple of diamonds for insurance, some family photos and all the resort clothes we can pack in two large suitcases. We'll live on a cruise ship like characters in a Scott Fitzgerald novel from the 1920s. We'll speak six languages and send postcards to all our family and friends. "*Ciao,* darlings," I will write as we debark at Venice, and "*Je t'adore*!" as we wait for our plane at Orly. Everyone will think our lives are *tres* glamorous and I'll never wash another dish, *vraiment!*

"Have you priced any cruises this year? my conscience asks.

When I am old I might emulate the strong Native American women of the New World. I will find a cabin on the coast of Newfoundland that faces the sea, catch our food on fishing lines in a nearby cove and broil my catch over an open fire. The wind will blow strong from the sea, the moon will play chase with ragged clouds and the surf will pound against the cliffs. Every night Dick will build a roaring fire in the big rock fireplace in our cabin and we will roll up in sleeping bags on the floor and sleep in front of the fire. I will never wear pantyhose again, when I am old and living in Newfoundland.

"You always were such an outdoor girl."

Well then, I'll be a Southern gentlewoman. We will rescue a derelict antebellum mansion with a rank of trees leading down an overgrown drive to a vine-covered pillared porch. When I am old, Dick and I will renovate the mansion. We'll keep blooded horses in the stables and raise our own chickens for frying. We'll hold charity bazaars on the grounds of the historic old place and all our neighbors will be dazzled by our style and delighted to see the old plantation lively again.

"Who's going to sing 'My Old Kentucky Home,' honey Chile?"

On the other hand, when I am old I could be an astronaut. When John Glenn was old he went up in space again as a sort of experimental monkey and the doctors put him through a lot of tests to see what space travel does to old men. I never heard the results, but I would like to know. So I will be the old woman astronaut. Think of the headlines! I'll write a book about it and the screenplay will star Vanessa Redgrave and Dick and I will make a lot of money and keep some of it and give the rest to the poor.

"In his 70s John Glenn could run a six-minute mile, climb stairs like a cat, his blood pressure was 120/40 and I don't want to hear about his cheekbones."

Never mind. When I am old I'll write a book about my quirky but delightful parents and my quiet and thoughtful childhood and sign my books everywhere on a tour of the United States. I'll wear a little black dress with a single strand of real pearls and a simple diamond watch. In New York my publishers will put me up at The Plaza and in Dallas at The Adolphus. There will be champagne and flowers in my suites, white tulips in a crystal vase, and I will dine where international chefs do all the cooking.

"Written any good books lately?"

Or maybe when I am old I'll become a hippy. We'll sell our house, I'll let my hair grow below my waist, buy a pair of torn jeans and sing in the shower about yellow submarines. Dick will wear a hat from the Australian outback and we'll put on hiking boots and lots of turquoise jewelry and visit each of our five children for two months every year and disappear for the remaining two months, hitching rides and blowin' in the wind. We'll take street cars and buses and talk to all the people who never saw a McMansion. We won't carry anything and all we'll own is the clothes we stand up in.

"And the turquoise jewelry, of course. The trouble is you're missing the point."

What point?

"I hate to be indelicate, but you're already old."

That's not only indelicate, it's inaccurate. I've never bought a blue crepe dress, or visited Newfoundland, or broken the sound barrier or learned the words to "Yellow Submarine." I've just started looking for a literary agent and it's going to take me a couple of years to run all this by Dick. Listen up, my friend. Like the poet says, you'd better string along with me. The best hasn't even started yet.

COUNTRY ROADS HAVE TALES TO TELL

As this year's rock hard winter runs its course and green shoots begin to push up through cold ground, long-traveled animal trails are easy to track in Missouri's spring woodland. Our dog Bandit for years raced out the front door every morning, cantered east up a bank and over the road into the steep, deep woods. Bandit is gone now two years, yet the trail he blazed, growing fainter with time, remains a testimony to his seeking spirit.

In early America, European settlers, bewildered by the vastness of their new home, followed animal trails because they often led to lifesaving water on a long trek, or proved a short cut to a destination. Natural trails, cut into the land by the feet of repeated users and modified by human need, come in all shapes and sizes, often bearing little resemblance to their origins. Glittering Broadway in New York City was once a trail beaten down by the hooves of cattle ambling from pasture to barn. Great rivers are themselves watery trails, thoroughfares pioneers adopted where forest land was impenetrable. Early travelers were likely, too, to find settlements of people like themselves along the rivers where water was plentiful and transportation as close as the nearest mooring.

Long before covered wagons rumbled through tall-grass prairies across Missouri, pioneers poled into this untamed territory on Missouri River craft. Had the river cut deeper into its channel at the site of the early Boone County settlements of Claysville and Nashville, those thriving commercial cities might still stand as important trading complexes where goods landed for distribution to the interior. But Old Man River cut himself a new highway that carried the cities away.

The town of Ashland thrived because it stood at the corner of a major north/south trail that first became Highway 63 and in the late 1960s expanded to a four-lane high-speed commuter route of the same name. Rice's Garage, which long stood at the corner of Henry Clay Boulevard and Old Highway 63 in Ashland, was the mid-journey gasoline stop for early automobiles traveling between Columbia and the state capital at Jefferson City before "the Slab," as locals called the concrete four-lane, was built.

Mention Ashland to the native-born and you'll hear about Rice's. The land the little service station stood on is still a prime location, the site of a modern gas station and convenience store. Who knows what "conveniences" Rice's offered? The town's late memoirist, John Pauley, said when he was a kid he would ride his bike to Rice's in the hot summertime for ice cream cones and cold soda pop.

Ashland's earliest initiative, after the town was founded in 1875, was to try to attract a railroad. It seemed reasonable to the founders, and it seems reasonable today, that a railroad running from the river cities north through Ashland to the city of Columbia and connecting north to Centralia's main line, was good for business. But the venture failed to carry a citizen vote, a failure that forecast the city's destiny.

Railroads were king in the late 1800s, long before Henry Ford dreamed of assembly lines and ages before President Dwight Eisenhower encouraged the building of intercontinental highways. Virtually all early major commerce was by river barge and railroad. Ashland's position, five miles from the river and just off the railroad, doomed it to remain a quiet, rural backwater until tractor/trailer trucks from the four-lane highway brought consumer goods, boards for buildings and rapid growth to the area. The little town slumbered till highway builders blasted through hill and prairie to link the town with its major central Missouri neighbors.

Traveling concrete highways, if you keep your eyes open, can have more meaning than simply getting there. Look for the signs of earlier roads the highway subsumed (in part) as its own. Watch for the off ways of dirt roads and tracks that disappear into fields and woodland.

Across northern Boone County you'll find, under and alongside existing roads, traces of the Boonslick Trail, the great wagon road that led those who were westward bound to the Santa Fe, California and Oregon Trails. The Boonslick is the trail our ancestors and their oxen made by habitually going over the same ground. Like all trails, it demonstrates both a practical direction and a defined purpose.

In the late winter and early-spring woods, if you turn off the blacktop and follow clear or faint byways, they are likely to reveal why they are there. Some were old roads tracing the shortest distance between two points. Other paths led to a source of life-giving water. Fading tracks once showed a family the way to go home. At trail's end you may find scattered bricks that mark an abandoned house site, with a lilac tree still blooming where once a doorway opened on warmth and welcome.

In the next month or so these traveled ways will stand out more clearly, lanes threading bare ground through burgeoning spring growth, marking our ancient ways of passing. These beaten paths have their own purpose, their miles to go, and although their history may be lost in the gauzy fogs of spring, following long-used, well-traveled trails will lead you wherever your reverie chooses to roam.

An Urgency Of Surrender

Along a winding country road in North Carolina we found a haunted place one winter day, a place disassembled by time and recreated whole with the aura of every spirit intact. A small farm house set in the fragrance of the piney woods where a great Civil War general chose to deliver up his army, and Nancy Bennett, a Carolina farm woman, surrendered to the force of her destiny.

In April 1865 it's likely, as William Vatavuk writes, that the woods around Bennett Place "were afire with blooming dogwood and redbud, while in the fields and meadows upland cress, wild azalea, and honeysuckle sprang from the stiff, red soil…"

On small farms like the 200 acres James Bennett worked, April passes in quick time. James was in the fields on a day in mid April of 1864, while Nancy Bennett and their widowed daughter, Eliza Bennett Duke, tended the house and Eliza's children. Bennett land hadn't been fought over like the farmland of the Shenandoah Valley or the fields around Gettysburg or that wide swath from Atlanta to the sea. But recently some 40,000 outnumbered Confederate troops had thundered north along the Hillsborough Road that ran close to the farmhouse, deftly retreating from a Union Army investing Raleigh. They must have left behind a whisper of unease in the dust they raised in passing, the sense of momentous happenings brewing.

The steep-sloped roof of the small clapboard farmhouse covers three rooms, a working fireplace and a crooked bank of stairs leading to a sleeping loft. Standing in Nancy Bennett's parlor it's possible to imagine that you hear hoof beats, distant at first, the approach of a cavalcade of horses. But these horses don't pass by and suddenly, framed in a parlor window, there's a world of horses, the farmyard crowded with hundreds of men on horseback, men wearing blue uniforms and gray, spurs jingling, leather rasping, horses neighing, blowing and stamping, men calling to each other. Do the women stand frozen with fear? Do they grab up small children and hold them close? When the knock comes at the door and Nancy goes to open it a soldier says, "Excuse me, ma'am, but you will have to leave. General Johnston and General Sherman need to make use of your parlor."

The mounted men numbered near 500, the aides and staffs of the Confederate and Union generals. A week and a day earlier, General Robert E. Lee had surrendered the Army of Northern Virginia to General U. S. Grant at Appomattox. On this day, Union General W. T. Sherman's heart was heavy with news he shared only with Johnston: President Abraham Lincoln had been assassinated the day before the generals met. General Joseph Johnston had troubles of his own, factions in the fleeing Confederate government commanding him never to surrender. Split your forces, they said, and send guerilla bands throughout the nation to keep the conflict alive.

But the Confederacy's ranking general, like Sherman a proud West Point graduate, arranged instead to ride south on the Hillsborough Road while Sherman rode north until the two parties ran into each other and Johnston mentioned he had just passed a small farmhouse where they might sit together and discuss the terms of surrender. And so they came to Bennett Place and knocked on Nancy's door and the women and children gathered up their things and fled to a kitchen outbuilding where the wait proved longer than they had expected.

The generals met in Nancy's parlor three times before they hammered out a surrender and with it, a lifelong friendship. The ultimate agreement that Johnston and Sherman signed on April 26, 1865, led to the end of hostilities as unit by unit, remaining Confederate forces lay down their arms.

You reach Bennett Place on a two-lane blacktop that still leads to Hillsborough, but the old Hillsborough Road runs closer to the farmhouse door and now forms the path rimmed by stacked-wood fencing that leads you from the visitors' center to the farmhouse yard. Docents at Bennett Place will tell you that this surrender site carries more weight even than Appomattox. Lee's army was starving, they say, out of ammunition, surrounded. But Johnston's surrender was a principled choice, an act that brought a "Dawn of Peace" not merely to a state but to a war-weary nation.

The benefits of peace were a long time coming for Nancy and James Bennett. They lost two sons and a son-in-law to the war and when the peace process was over and the last trooper rode free of their gate, they looked on a scene of desolation. Both armies had turned their horses loose in the Bennett fields, made off with livestock, helped themselves to anything that caught their fancy. It took time to restore order after great men and the great armies they commanded – 140,000 troops in all – receded from their lives as grimly as they had arrived.

In a long life, was there ever a quiet spring day when Nancy Bennett didn't stop suddenly for a moment to listen? Did the splatter of redbuds in the spring woods bring back the sound of horses approaching, the noise of a world of horses in the farmyard, the officious knock at the door? This is the drama of Bennett Place, where a pair of great generals surrendered to peace and a farm woman named Nancy Bennett opened the door to her parlor and stepped into history.

Hear That Lonesome Whistle

I keep hoping the railroads will make a comeback in the United States. So far, they seem to be going in the other direction. J. P. Morgan was smart enough to make a fortune running railroads 100 years ago, and Europe and Japan still rely on modern fast rail. With most airlines beset by debt and the big names vanishing like clouds in a gale, there could be an opportunity for an entrepreneur to make fast rail an alternative, if he could just get all of us aboard.

A friend of mine told me she planned a trip to Chicago on Amtrak, and I whooped with pleasure. "What," she said, "you like railroads?" She's never traveled on a train, but I grew up with the lonesome wail of locomotives whistling in the night at a time when anybody who was going anywhere ran to catch the train.

Our family lived in one of many small New Jersey towns strung like beads along the tracks of the Erie and Lackawanna Railroad that fed commuters to and from New York City. In Ridgewood, my home town, the train station still stands in the center of town, looking the same today as it always did. There are tall iron fences and a gate, a small station house with a red-tiled roof and a lawn with green grass and round evergreen shrubs. Being there is like taking a virtual tour of the station in a model train setup.

Every summer, my family put me on a train on the Seaboard Line that snaked along the Atlantic coast. I boarded the train at Newark where the giant engines came snorting into the covered terminal like prehistoric creatures, pistons churning, steam hissing, bells ringing. When I stepped on board one of the passenger cars I was on my way to Charlotte, North Carolina for my annual summer visit with my aunts and uncles.

The daily commuter trains my dad rode to work were a study in minimalism. But the long distance trains were sleek and luxurious, with soft upholstery, tilt-back chairs in the coaches and art-deco designs on the end panels. The dining cars are legendary for their snow white tablecloths, perfect service and great food. You could always get plenty of exercise on a long train ride, walking from coach to coach. Eventually you'd get to the plushy Observation Car and you could sit at a table and have something to drink and look out the rear windows at the tracks melting away behind you. The way I traveled wasn't top of the line, but when my dad left on a cross-country trip (as he did often) he'd book a compartment with a sitting room, bedroom and bath. He knew the names of most of the conductors on the major trains across America.

Dad was crazy about trains and it was contagious. He boarded the commuter train every morning that he was at home but that didn't keep him from driving down to the station in the evening after dinner a couple of times a week, taking me along. He would park the car and we would sit there and watch the long lines of freight cars making their soft clicking noises as they passed by with the names of the railroads written on their sides. "Look at that," my dad would say. "There's a

Great Northern right next to a Santa Fe. Think how far they've come!" On the way home we would stop for ice cream.

My last long railroad journey was when I left home for college in Minnesota. My ticket was on the famed Chicago Limited with a transfer to the Burlington Line for Minneapolis. Burlington pioneered a double-decker car called a Vista Dome with a roof like a glass bubble. I climbed the stairs to the observation deck and sat there watching with wide-open Eastern eyes as the great Midwest unfolded all around me.

Fast trains still operate from city to city in the Northeast. But the crack streamliners that ran from New York to Chicago and San Francisco are long gone, trains that broke time barriers and bore names of their own.

For years a small group of enthusiasts have tried to get fast rail between St. Louis and Kansas City. About 10 years ago they sponsored the visit of a prototype European train that ran the route. Newspaper editors were invited to go along. The train was a marvel of efficiency, available for sale to the state of Missouri, and the price was right. I talked to the train's designer and asked him about the condition of our tracks. The tracks are no problem, he told me. It's the communications systems that are sadly out of date. He said in Europe, it's all done by computers. Missouri could have bought one of those trains, but it never happened.

For a long time I've dreamed of taking the Trans-Canada Railroad, or The Flying Scot from London to Edinburgh, or the Orient Express, all among the famous trains of the world. America has no famous trains anymore.

Just for the joy of it, now and then Dick and I book a ticket on Amtrak from Jefferson City to Kansas City to visit our kids, just so we can sit back and enjoy the ride. At the historic capital city terminal, we wait for the big diesel engine to come whistling round the bend. The old steam engines were more romantic, but all train engines radiate power. Inside the cars to Kansas City and St. Louis, Amtrak is not as minimalist as the old Erie and Lackawanna commuter trains and not as luxurious as the fabled streamliners.

For relaxing travel it's hard to beat a train, almost any train, clicking over the rails past a back-country landscape you can't see from the road or the sky. As the landscape reels by outside the wide windows of an Amtrak coach, travel by train can bring Arcadia to Missouri, if you can imagine that.

VACATION PREPARATION

Getting ready to go on a journey is no picnic. Even when you know three months in advance where you're going and have your airline tickets in your hand, the last couple of days before you leave are always hectic.

There are all kinds of journeys in our lives. Leaps of faith. Losing oneself in a good book. Passages from young adult to middle age to retirement. Any steep learning curve is a journey and relationships almost always lead us down some primrose path. All journeys have value, but there are times when there is nothing quite like simply getting out of town.

Knowing three months in advance that you're going on vacation is a help because it gives you time to go on a diet. Three months ahead seems such a long time that it invites procrastination and you're inclined to say, "Oh, a little ice cream can't hurt in the long run." So you spend the last five days before you leave eating one egg for breakfast, one piece of sandwich meat for lunch and skipping dinner. It doesn't work and you know that, but you do it anyway.

Dick came in the door last week wearing a wide smile and carrying a large bundle. "Look what I found!" he chortled. "Fresh sweet corn – in June!" The sweet corn came from Florida so it was what you might call proto-fresh, but it had several days' jump on anything you'd find in most grocery store produce counters.

"I'm so sorry," I said. "I'm dieting, so I am not eating sweet corn this week." He couldn't believe it. He has always considered himself lucky that I crave fresh sweet corn more than I long for diamonds. "No sweet corn, beans, bread, potatoes, cereal, pasta or sugar," I said sternly. So he telephoned the kids who live nearby and invited them for dinner, muttering that he'd rather be married to a person who would eat sweet corn with him than some skinny woman.

It takes a lot of planning to go on vacation. I've been combing through my clothes for months. You don't want to take your ordinary, everyday clothes on vacation. You want to take things that are relatively new and make you look thin, with the right shoes and earrings. The inventory is alarming.

We are going to North Carolina and in that place I don't worry about gaps in my wardrobe, because my peppy little daughter-in-law would rather shop than eat (and has the figure to prove it). "I can pick up anything I need after I get there," I tell myself.

Then I discover I'm out of shampoo and I need a small toothpaste and a new pair of slip-on shoes to wear to the airport so when they tell you to take your shoes off it's no big thing. You wind up doing a lot of running around, because although shopping is often a girl thing that includes lunch, you usually shop for intimate apparel by yourself. And no matter how diligent you've been with your diet you know you can't fake it when days at the beach are on the itinerary, so you spend hours trying on bathing suits and looking for a cover-up that doesn't make you look like your husband is a member of the Taliban.

Trying to get some sleep just before you leave isn't easy either. I close my eyes to visions of a plane in flight. A conglomeration of computer technology and mechanization that reason tells me can't possibly fly. I've never boarded an airplane without a gut feeling that this bucket of bolts will (a) never get off the ground or (b) never stay airborne unless I keep a steady upward pressure on the armrests. There aren't many atheists in airplanes. I pray as hard as anybody else and though I'm not Catholic, I throw in a few Hail Marys. "Pray for us sinners now and at the hour of our death," is a logical sort of prayer for a passenger in an airplane who's looking to cover all the bases.

By the time you actually start putting clothes into a suitcase you wonder why you didn't give all of it to the Goodwill instead. And do you want to under pack, or over pack? Travel light and trust to luck, or add a little something to cover every contingency?

A woman vice president of a major newspaper corporation was speaker at a press conference I chaired several years ago and I picked her up at the airport. She arrived for the weekend looking gorgeous in a silk pantsuit and carrying a single tote bag. I checked her the entire time for signs of meltdown but it never happened.

I've always wanted to travel hands-free like that but I've never come close. For our vacation we need to take beach clothes and everyday vacation clothes and clothes to go to the theater and out to dinner and to parties. You can't put all that in a tote bag. Besides, I'm always better off if I take a few things I never wear instead of finding I need something I can visualize hanging in my closet back home.

With the planning and the packing and the dieting and the flying, by the time I get where I'm going I spend the first two days of my vacation resting up. But this is not such a bad thing. Your host and hostess may be a little perplexed, but isn't resting up what vacations are all about?

The Romance Of Motoring

You can't improve on the view from the window of an automobile rolling along one of America's great highways. We hear a lot about cars and drivers these days, most of it negative. The SUVs are way too big. Gas consumption holds us hostage to foreign oil. Drivers are rude, there's too much speed, too much road rage, too many cell phones. And what are they doing, anyway, putting television screens in cars?

We forget to turn that coin over, delve into memories of the romance of the open road, something that's still there in spite of our best efforts to wipe it out. You can't help catching your breath at the approach to the Cumberland Gap where the road rises up out of the Kentucky flats into mist-shrouded gorges. Or go giddy with the joy of Summit, South Dakota where you cross the Continental Divide and from that high pinnacle, looking north, the world spreads out before you with a gentle curve at the horizon like the rim of a large dinner plate.

"Motoring," they called it when the automobile was new. Driving as a pastime, just to feel the wheels turning, listen to the thrum of the motor and see what was out there where the clamor of the cities ended and the randomness of the countryside began.

Interstate 70 girdles Missouri's midsection like a belt, bisecting the state's culture and climate. North of the beltline are softly undulating croplands that spread wider and higher into the Great Plains states. Almost immediately south, the flat land gives way to the corrugation of river bluffs and glacial valleys. These are the foothills of the Ozarks, the oldest mountains on the continent.

Missouri shares the temperate zone with such states as Connecticut and Georgia, and a plurality of plants that grow here also grow there. Yet on a particular day on a certain highway that rises seamlessly to meet a soaring blue sky, a highway bordered on either side by rolling grassland interrupted by woods and defined by streams, common enough in many states, that highway suddenly, undeniably, defines a Missouri landscape. Just as a similar road cutting through land in Connecticut or Georgia would be unmistakably typical of its homeland. Commerce may deliver a world knee deep in wrappers from the fast food at every tenth mile marker from coast to coast, but the romance of the road keeps time with the hum where the rubber meets the road.

There is a band of territory that begins at the Canadian border and ends at the states that ring the gulf of Mexico. We call it the Middle West, and East and West Coastal dwellers find something about the word "middle" that implies the banal if not the ridiculous. "The Midwest?" they say. "That's the place you fly over on the way from New York to Los Angeles." And I tell them they ought to drive it sometime, experience the landscape, feel the drone of vast distance, catch the romance. The coasts don't look so tempting themselves, viewed from an airplane window at 30,000 feet above a thick overlay of high clouds.

In the current era, the Midwest is at a stage of development a shade removed from the coasts and just now, a decade or so pleasanter. You can still drive a few miles at a stretch between the central hub city of Columbia, Missouri and the metropolis of Kansas City or St. Louis without sighting a billboard. You can still imagine, from your seat behind the wheel, that streams and small rivers winding off into the dark green mystery of overhanging trees, or a lonely barn rising like a monument to agriculture on a distant hill, peaceful and serene on a mild and cloudless day, are akin to the world as it was meant to be.

Which is not to say that the fingerprints of humankind are not there, even in the open country between the small towns that sprawl along Interstate 70. Settlers bridged the rivers, brought the fat cattle to graze on the fertile hillside around the barn, and probably built the barn from the wood of a primeval forest they cleared so they could crop the land and pasture the animals.

Drive any route in America and see shopping centers rising out of fallow bean fields. Housing developments and industrial parks gobble up farmland and wilderness, fill the countryside with the inevitable accessories of development – the billboard and the traffic interchange and the convenience store and the access road and the adult video shop and the fireworks stand. They accrue over periods of time, straw upon straw, but there is solace in knowing they are no more than surface toys that a team of bulldozers could scrape from the land in a matter of hours. It is always possible to replenish prairies and plant forests, if we are worthy of the work.

Roadways crisscross America – gravel roads, blue highways, toll roads, interstates and throughways. They lead you from farmhouse to town, from town to city, from city to city and all the places in between. They'll take you where canyon walls throw sharp shadows in the desert outside Santa Fe, where the blue undulations of the Great Smoky Mountains merge with the horizon, where rhythmic waves wash against an Atlantic shoreline, where tall firs reach for a sky reflected in a cold Canadian lake. These are the views from the windows of your car when you take to the open road. Call it motoring. Better yet, call it romance.

The Unfriendly Skies

It was hard to believe nobody was killed when a passenger plane skidded off a runway recently. In spite of a couple of failed emergency exits, the air crew succeeded in getting everyone on the ground before the ship went up in flames .In our ordinary world, chaos can strike without warning, creating a once-in-a-million disaster. The unfriendly skies seem to attract chaos, which is why I decided a long time ago that the wild blue yonder can be way too wild for my comfort zone.

When it was all over, airport officials wondered if the runway at that airport shouldn't be lengthened, and if maybe they ought to fill in the deep ravine at the end of it. I couldn't help thinking about the many times I've flown into LaGuardia in New York City, where the drop-off at the end of a short runway is water – a whole lot of water. For a while there, planes were dunking their noses into the water at LaGuardia on a regular basis, one of them just before an assignment took me to North Carolina and on to New York. It was early morning as we flew along the river. A bright sun made every Manhattan skyscraper window wink gold, a glorious sight, But the short runway was still uppermost in my mind.

I fell in love with flying in its early days when long flights were still a luxury. Around 1950, I left Geneva after a summer in Switzerland to fly to Paris, where I picked up my return flight to London. A thunderstorm struck over the Alps and the plane, a four-engine Continental, was dropping into air pockets and rising again and lightning was flashing all around us and I was no more frightened than if I had been on a roller coaster at Palisades Park. We left Paris for London at 3 a.m. in another spacious Connie with only about nine other passengers who promptly went to sleep. The Air France pilots were on a routine flight and they were bored. So they sent a steward to invite me to the cockpit and I sat on a jump seat between them so they could show the American girl the English Channel at night. It was some sight from that big glass bubble, with the lights of fishing boats on the water far below twinkling like the stars above. I chatted with the French captains and it seemed a short time before I caught a glimpse of the city of London spread out like all the jewels from Aladdin's cave. But when the pilots began the serious countdown that brings the plane safely to the ground, I was politely ushered back to my seat.

At a time when planes were far less safe than they are today, I wanted to fly everywhere. I boarded a DC-3, a relic of World War II, and flew from New York City to North Bay, Ontario to visit friends. Later, I took every opportunity to fly in Cessnas of any size. Once I found a pilot who agreed to circle the spire of the Church of St. Mary in Fulton, Missouri so I could hang out the window to photograph the Churchill Memorial from the top down. I needed the illustration for a story I was writing.

It had been several years since I had flown when I booked passage on my first 727 passenger jet from St. Louis to New York to visit my family. I felt something alien about that plane from the minute I slipped into the skinny little seat. A longtime aviation stalwart, I was suddenly a white-knuckled coward. I said to myself, "I am going to die. I know it." Tears streamed down my face as I thought of my motherless children. A kind man in a business suit sat down next to me. "Are you all right?" he asked. "Can I help?" I didn't know what to say. We weren't off the ground yet.

There is no logic in my fear of the friendly skies. Unfortunately, it won't go away. I say unfortunately because it's hard to get some places – Hawaii, for instance – unless you fly. My son-in-law Randy flew the F-16 and the Stealth fighter for the U. S. Air Force and now flies commercially because he would rather pilot an airplane – any airplane – than eat. He counsels me. "Look at it this way," he says. "I'm a pilot. It's my life, too. Would I be up there if I thought it was dangerous?" I appreciate his kindness, but you have to admit fighter pilots don't see danger the way you and I do. His next argument rang a bell, though. When you're flying from Kansas City to North Carolina, he said, think about this: You're on the air crew's regular run. They do this all the time. To them, it's the day job.

Every time I fly I swear it's the last time, but it never is. Since my talk with Randy, I have a new strategy that helps keep panic at bay. I ask the stewards or stewardesses what they plan to do when they land. Are they going home? Out to a favorite restaurant? I reason if they've made plans to get on with their lives, I can do that too.

On a recent flight my stewardess tells me she loves my jacket and she is going to drop in at Chico's in Raleigh tomorrow morning to see if she can find one like it. Tomorrow, this girl is going to the mall, going to park her car and walk on solid ground in the tar-heel state. Surely chaos must be off causing trouble somewhere else if the stewardess is going to Chico's.

I listen for the clunk of the wheel gear (that's good, the wheels are down). I pray for a safe landing and receive in response a measure of calm. "Let's be logical here," I tell myself as I gather up my belongings and step into the aisle that leads to the open door. "I've lived a long life and I have never done a once-in-a-million anything. Chaos or no chaos, it's pretty unlikely that's going to change." How easy it is to put chaos back in its bottle when your aircraft rests comfortably on the ground.

Hawaii, My Love

This winter we'll make our fifth trip to the Hawaiian Islands, back to the north shore of Oahu where the Resort at Turtle Bay stands on a spit of land thrust into the wild Pacific. From the resort grounds you look out over an ocean so vast and deep you feel the surf thrumming under your feet. The sea spans 4,000 uninterrupted miles to the islands of Japan. The north beach is where we stand and watch the "white horses" of sea spray and salt spume riding turbulent waves that crash at our feet and drain away into the sand.

I was 12 years old when I first read "The Black Camel" by Earl Derr Biggers, an old book I pulled down from my dad's library shelves. Biggers wrote, "Exotic flowers, blooming trees, verdant green hills, blue, sunny skies with billowy white clouds – the whole a dream of the unchanging tropics." Reading his words, I fell head over heels in love with Hawaii. It was to be many years before my travels taught me that the author's prose was accurate. The Hawaiian Islands never disappoint.

Biggers introduced Detective Charlie Chan to the world of literature, radio and film. Charlie starred in several books written in the 1920s when Hawaii drew vacationing mainlanders to a paradise of beautiful people, pineapples and palm trees. Biggers wrote with all the flair of the flapper era, those shimmering years that ended in the Great Depression. He was not a literary giant in the style of F. Scott Fitzgerald, but you find echoes of his breezy prose in the work of O. Henry and some of the short stories of Jack London. London's love of the islands was so intense that he and his wife built a boat on the California coast and sailed it to Hawaii where he wrote a fistful of evocative stories before his untimely death.

When we first meet Charlie Chan, he is a sergeant of police in Honolulu, the proud father of 11 children, the owner of a house on Punchbowl Hill. His success elevates him to the rank of Inspector by the time the black camel kneels at the gate of movie star Shelah Fane on Kealakekua Avenue, stabbed to death in a rented mansion while her guests sip cocktails on the lanai overlooking Waikiki Beach.

When the call comes for him to investigate the murder, Inspector Chan is contemplating the fish course at a Rotary dinner at the Royal Hawaiian Hotel, the elegant pink palace that still represents the best of Waikiki. Biggers gave the famous landmark an alias, "The Grand Hotel," but when he writes of the view from the echoing central hallway looking toward the beach through "three great arches framing a tropic sky," readers know exactly where they are. Walking the avenue to the scene of the murder, Charlie's progress gives the author a chance to lament the onset of progress: "On this tiny island in the midst of the rolling Pacific, few outward signs of a romantic past survived…a trolley clattered by, he walked on a concrete sidewalk under the soft yellow glow of modern street lamps. Yet beyond the range of those lamps he was conscious of the black velvet of the tropic night. He caught the odor of ginger blossoms and plumeria, a croton hedge gave way to one of hibiscus topped with pale pink flowers that were doomed to die at midnight." At Shelah Fane's door, Charlie passes "beneath a prolific banyan tree, two centuries older than the motion pictures."

Biggers never lets up. A young Chamber of Commerce booster named Jimmy Bradshaw supplies the novel's love interest, wooing a dark-haired beauty with violet eyes by reciting the delights of his island home: "The climate breeds happiness and laughter, a natural reflection of the sunlight, the rainbows and the purple hills…Honolulu has its message of beauty for every heart."

Biggers' words so enchanted me that I sought Hawaii stories all my life, building a towering dream of aloha-land that meshed and melded and became entangled in my own heart's messages of beauty when we first traveled to the islands in 1996. Since then we've returned every second year, exploring Kauai's ancient canals, sweet gardens and small town living; Maui, with its luxury resorts and wild coastline on the road to Hana; Oahu, glamorous home of the city of Honolulu and Waikiki beach; and the Big Island of Hawaii where the cold cracked surface of old volcanic flows and the steaming red death of hot lava from Mauna Kea are constant reminders of the newness and impermanence of these isolated land masses.

On the island of Oahu, "the gathering place," in the city of Honolulu, progress is such that we can only wish for the days of the trolley cars and the gentle glow of the "modern street lamps" Biggers deplores.

Today's visitors, disconnected from the native villages that existed in the 1920s, find their history on Honolulu's echoing wharves, drawing dream pictures of the bustle there when Charlie Chan patrolled the city and the great Matson ocean liners came and went. Passengers tossed streams of confetti from luxury ships to the receding shore. Leaving the islands for the mainland, they threw flowered leis into the sea to assure their return to paradise.

From the wharves today you look inland up Charlie's Punchbowl Hill and the peaks beyond and see a counterpane of construction, apartment buildings merging with subdivisions marching up the mountains. This city, like others in America that live with quick-buck decisions poorly executed, has its ill-kept neighborhoods where wastepaper tumbles on trade winds through grimy streets. But there's a special excitement in Honolulu, an Asian rim metropolis where Japanese, Chinese, Filipino and Portuguese laborers arrived in waves through history to work the cane and pineapple fields. Most of them stayed to establish the melting pot that is the island signature.

In Waikiki where Shelah Fane lived and died, the sidewalks are as wide as country roads. On any given day you see dapper Asian businessmen strolling the avenue in $800 Hawaiian shirts, young women executives carrying briefcases tapping along briskly in stiletto heels, pairs of youngsters with tangled hair in bathing suits and flip-flops toting surfboards, and all the tourists in the world. At night tall tiki torches light storefronts and the faces of the people passing by. Hawaii, my love.

In Waikiki I drank champagne in the lounge of the pink palace with its soaring triple arches, tramped Kealakekua's sidewalks past a public beach where chess players gathered small audiences in clean swept shelter houses. Red ti plants rustling under blossoming plumerias separated the sidewalk from the beach. The ocean at Waikiki is so buoyant I lay on the water or hugged my knees to my chest, drifting on the current past all the grand hotels. Biggers and countless others write fluently of "silken surf beating on coral sand" under "the pastel loveliness of a lunar rainbow." We find in these islands too a culture that ennobles friendliness and caring. The primitive native villages are gone, but the spirit of aloha lives on, a dominant force in daily island living.

Viewed in the brilliant freshness of a sunny day or the black velvet of the tropic night, Oahu's flagship city shares with every visitor the aura of all its colorful pasts. Towering dream builder that I am, I imagine one thing more: that pressed into some Honolulu sidewalk there remain the time-eroded, faint outlines of the fictional footsteps of Inspector Charlie Chan.

Late Winter Journey

In late winter the ground is still snow-covered along our shaded cove and the lake a spreadng sheet of milky ice. In an average winter, lakewater reflects high clouds and the occasional sleepy path of winter sun, a foil for crystal days when all the earth is white. But this was no ordinary winter. Snow came early, made friends with the icy air, and stayed. It's become old snow now, showing its age in its dubious color, like the scuffed white shoes of children who have stayed too long at the party.

Even in a winter as cold as this one, patches of spring-fed water leave clear pools in the ice and Canada geese find them, fly down and arrange themselves in noisy circles around the icy rims, convening like board members at a conference table. On cold mornings when the earth is quiet and still, they all talk at once, barking their welcome to each new day. In late winter the cold skies sing with a new high keening. Driving along the snow-speckled plain of the Missouri River valley, I see necklaces of geese flung across the sky, their flight patterns merging, spreading, lenghtening like strings of beads stirred by a careless hand.

From ground level across our road and up the hill into the woods, wide waterfalls of thick icicles still cascade over limestone outcroppings, beginning to change shape as the weather warms, growing inch by inch narrower and drop by drop longer till they break and shatter on the rocks below. Winter is waning, its muted landscape of gray and taupe, black and white, pierced last week by flocks of restless robins, hundreds of them, flashing red and black through tree branches at eye level from our screen porch. Watching them we feel winter's embrace letting go. Like the robins, after a hard winter, we celebrate temperatures hovering in the 40s. Just a week or so ago when we left the house we buttoned coats snugly to the neck and pulled on boots and layered gloves. These days our coats fly open over sweaters. We still need boots, but tuck gloves into baskets where they'll wait, if we're lucky, for the cold of another winter.

Poet Percy Shelley, that great chronicler of the seasons, treats us to a virtual late winter journey:

"I dreamed that, as I wandered by the way,
Bare Winter suddenly was changed to Spring,
And gentle odours led my steps astray,
Mixed with the sound of water's murmuring…"

February isn't entirely alien to the gentle odors and murmuring water of spring, but this year, while we may be on our way to Babylon, our feet are mired in our own backyards. No change of season inspires more soul searching than spring as we gather up our dry and bony selves and propel them out of houses we've made sanctuaries. We can't quite grasp the reality of bright blue bachelor buttons or sweet-smelling roses, but stacks of seed catalogs lead us to dreams of picture-perfect gardens. As night cold comes down hard after a day warmed by sun, we sit around the fire, seeing in the flames visions of our springtime selves, vowing day by day to throw off the constraints of winter as we drop layers of heavy clothes, remembering (as the fire warms our faces) what it's like to slip into shorts and a T-shirt and pad barefoot into a gentle morning. Maintenance is the order of the day, we reflect – on our rusty limbs, our minds, our bodies and our souls.

I spend an afternoon transferring stacks of winter's books to the bookshelves, placing them one by one, reflecting that if winter is a kind of imprisonment, and spring a parole, February is the season of preparedness. We live as if we were leaving on vacation, clearing our warmest clothes from our closets, bringing out a pair of cotton slacks to team with a sweater, beginning our countdown to Missouri's eternal promise of country roads edged in wildflowers.

At night I step out onto the deck, ignoring the dark and the distant sighing of the winter stars, straining to hear the first of the frog voices that will echo through sweet summer twilights, a memory as gauzy as a pinpoint of light glimpsed through the swirling whiteness of a snowstorm. This is our late winter journey, the bargain we make, to trade the miracle of snowflakes for the wonder of rebirth, of small green sprouts breaking earth in a quest, so like our own, for the solace of the sun.

Wilderness Beckons

In late afternoon I watch the patterns of lake water in our cove. On bright days the water is deep green with gold flashing over the crests of small waves, the colors blending and merging, changing patterns that reflect the heavy growth of trees along the shoreline. Just a few miles east of where I stand the road ends with the cleared land and true wilderness begins. There, in national park land, Cedar Creek spills over sun-washed rocks, flowing into pools that mirror the dark foliage of wild banks.

The lure of water and wild places lives in our consciousness. The earliest American settlers believed this land was blessed by Providence and still today, wilderness equates with godliness in the American heart. Few nations have set aside so many acres of untouched land, sacred places where wildlife is encouraged and industry restrained. Even in New York when early city leaders sought to establish a central park, the design created by landscape architect Frederick Law Olmstead was of broad meadows layered with banks of trees, an idealized vision of nature in the wild.

Hunters, hikers and trail enthusiasts seek wild places for refreshment and recreation, renewing their connectedness to the earth. Like most of us, I count my wilderness experience in hours, nothing longer.

I first entered the wild when I was five years old and my mother took me for a swim from a riverbank in northern Georgia. We lived in suburban Marietta and swam in the pool at our country club – why, then, the riverbank? From a distance the river was the soupy brown color of southern waterways. But when we waded laughing and splashing into the water, we found it clear and clean and we could see our feet on the pebbled bottom. Why the riverbank? Perhaps simply so I could experience a wild place at a time when accessible wild places were already growing rare.

My mother was not an "outdoor girl," but in the photo album she kept of her late teens and the early years of her marriage to my father, she pasted pictures of herself and her friends, laughing young people lolling on blankets in open fields or under trees along a creek or river, making faces at the camera. Picnicking in wild places was popular before and during the First World War and on into the 1920s. I find the same sort of pictures in biographies of my parents' peers, notably Scott and Zelda Fitzgerald, who seem to have picnicked often and in similar southern locales. By the time of my childhood, picnicking in the wild was something undertaken by Boy and Girl Scouts and the youth groups from churches.

Whatever my mother's purpose, that early dunk in wilderness water seems to have branded me for life. From a shoreline untenanted as far as the eye could see, on the spur of a moment on a day in June, a friend and I plunged and swam for a few freezing moments in icy Derwent Water in the Lake District of England. In Missouri's Ozarks after the opening day of trout season one year, Dick and I left the elbow-to-elbow crowds along the trout-rich streams and went in search of wilderness. Down a dirt road we found a wide, shallow river, pulled on our waders and walked its center line, casting our lures where there was no sound but the ripple of the water and the screams of outraged blue jays. The sun was warm on our shoulders and we came away with sunburn and contentment. No fish.

Later we took our children on wilderness treks in northern Arkansas far from the haunts of floaters and souvenir seekers, along gravel roads and grassy tracks, exploring creek beds and small rivers where aquatic creatures from minnows to crawdads flourished. We rarely flushed a fish big enough for a frying pan. At night, damply, we sought small clusters of cabins perched on rocky outcroppings with "Vacancy" signs out front, a variety of wayside inn once an American institution that seems now to have vanished from the earth.

Dick's brother's home in southwestern Missouri is not far from a pristine stream used by the neighborhood as a swimming hole. The branches of tall, old-growth trees meet above a wide creek that tumbles over rocks for miles, pooling at the foot of a bank where kids grab a long rope attached to a tree, swing high and drop squealing into deep water. There are no concession stands, bait shops or parking lots – just the neighbors' children and the shade of the trees, the gurgle of the creek, the complexities of rock and water patterns and the habitats of water creatures. Pleasures enough.

In his book, *Second Nature,* Michael Pollan writes, "For many of us nature is a last bastion of certainty; wilderness… is one of the last of our fast-dwindling supply of metaphysical absolutes, those comforting transcendental values by which we have traditionally taken our measure and set our sights."

From our deck at treetop level I view woods enough and water enough to call up my limited wilderness experience. There is meditation in the restless water of this lake and wisdom in the voice of these trees. If as Pollan says there is certainty in the spirit of nature, it is comforting that it is a spirit so compatible on slight acquaintance – an old, old spirit, strong and unassailable and long at work in this land.

Chapter Five: Roots and Ties

Parents Pass It On

Two things guide us through the puzzle of parenting: the advice of experts who write articles and books, and the behaviors our parents taught us. Of the two, the second is the potent one. We think we're raising our children, but in fact the wisdom of our grandparents is the basis of it all.

When my sisters and I arrived my mother and dad taught us the rules they learned from their Victorian parents. In this new century, I pass some of them on to my grandchildren; old basic teachings as good as gold.

It used to be that parents ruled by fiat, their absolute authority backed by the schools and the law. The worst of this structure could be cruelty to children who had little recourse. The best of it was that it allowed children to be children. When we were little kids, my mother chose our food, our clothes and our friends, set clocks to govern our days and standards for our behavior. We had two responsibilities: to show respect to adults and do our schoolwork to the best of our abilities. It was accepted that beyond that we were fully, delightfully and inventively carefree.

In a phone conversation with my eldest sister recently we agreed that we were lucky in our choice of parents. "They did what people of their time were so good at," she said. "They did their job." My psychologist sister is retired from oversight of child welfare for the state of New Jersey, giving her reason enough to heap praise on parents who step up to their work.

I wish I had listened more closely to my mother, who was so unfailingly wise. She taught us never to feel sorry for ourselves and never to burden family or friends with our troubles – they have enough of their own. She taught us to accept responsibility, say please and thank you and learn to govern our tempers, because an adult having a tantrum looks like such a fool. She said if we did something wrong (and everyone does) we should never let pride keep us from saying "I'm sorry."

My dad taught us to work hard, stand tall and live confidently. There was nothing we couldn't do, he said (given our health and intelligence), if we wanted to do it badly enough. He scorned cuss words as evidence that the speaker was too stupid to use the language. He said if a thing is not worth doing well, it's not worth doing at all. He said that he, himself, was not perfect, but that was no reason not to pay attention to what he said.

The rest he left to my mother, who was encouraged as a child to lead a clean and healthy life because our bodies are gifts from God. You honor others, she said, when you dress neatly. Sloppiness shows you have no respect for yourself or anybody else and innocent bystanders shouldn't have to look at a sorry sight like you. Live with dignity, she said, with consideration for the people around you, and with joy. Regardless of pain or misfortune, remember that being cheerful is a duty too.

Only cowardly people, my mother taught us, are rude to a salesclerk, a servant, a waitress or anyone else who can't answer back without putting their job in jeopardy. Laziness was forbidden at home and illness, though treated efficiently (my mother was a doctor's daughter, after all) was never an excuse. Only on your death bed could you be forgiven for failing to wash your face and comb your hair. There was no coughing, sneezing or nose blowing at the dinner table. We had the option of not doing those things, or taking our food in our rooms.

Lessons were everywhere. Abraham Lincoln was right to walk miles to return a few pennies he owed. The amount was not important; the principle of keeping your word was everything. The bishop in the book *Les Miserables* was doing God's work when he gave the silver candlesticks to the thief who was about to steal them. The bishop set an example of generosity and by forestalling a crime, helped save the thief's soul.

My son asked recently that his parents pass on hints to help him with the job of rearing two small sons. I was thinking of that last night, wondering what to tell him, when I stepped out on the deck where the moon shone full and neighbors' windows threw bands of light on the surface of the lake like arms outstretched in friendship.

We live today in a world so different from the world of my childhood it's beyond calculation what my parents and grandparents would make of this new century. But does it matter whether it's this century or that? Doesn't history teach us that there are truths that transcend time and place?

The night was very still. In spring there's hardly a hum from peepers and bullfrogs that in deep summer fill the dark with chorus. Arms resting on the deck railing, I was enjoying sight without sound when a faint crump-crump began in the distance, gradually growing louder as the lights of a single airplane came into view and arced leisurely overhead.

Our house is just off the flight path of the commuter planes from St. Louis, homeward bound to Columbia Regional Airport. I like the rare sighting of that lonely light crossing the sky and the homely churn of the engines that links me to passengers gathering up belongings before landing, while I stand alone on a deck on a lake in the woods and watch them pass overhead like the gods and goddesses in the chariots of ancient Greece.

The charted course of those daily flights varies no more than the path wisdom takes in its journey from grandparent to parent to child. How good are the ageless links to mothers and fathers, grandmothers and grandfathers, who lived in times we like to think were wiser than our own, whose ultimate goal was to leave the world a better place than they found it. Parents who did their jobs. They left us strength for our weaknesses, light for our darkness, legacies to cherish and ambitions to aspire to, gifts with the power to span centuries as we pass them on.

The Art Of Visiting

My daughter Kay and great-granddaughter Madison came to visit one day in spring. They brought me bouquets of roses, a large vase of hot pink blooms named "Valencia" and a small one of light red roses with flirty petals called "Majolica" and I put the roses on tables and we stood back and admired them.

A sweet light rain fell softly among the tracery of green branches outside the hearth room's wall of windows and a violin concerto played in the background. I brought out the "tiny toys" for Madi to look over while Kay and I caught up on family news. The tiny toys are thumbnail-size objects I've accumulated over the years and keep in a crystal and silver box – the sort of box children are usually told not to touch. Inside, there's an inch-high crystal Santa; a shoe token and a flat iron from an old Monopoly game, a tiny carved wooden soldier, a Mickey Mouse mask. a painted wooden bear, a glass penguin and other odd items – miniature things just right for a five-year-old to finger over and dream on. Madi sat on a cushion on the floor that made the big coffee table just the right height to lay out her treasures.

Afternoon visits have been absent from my life through all my career years, so I concentrate on the gift of their grace. Instinctively I hark back to times long past, bringing out blue willow plates, slicing pound cake, decorating the plates with swirls of chocolate and pouring glasses of lemonade. In my childhood, I can't remember a visit to the homes of my aunts when dessert wasn't served. But the great joy at Aunt Miriam's house was when she would take down a tiny gold tea set that I was allowed to play with only on special occasions. Whenever I see a child's tea set at an antique booth I think of the cherry pie with a lattice crust that my aunt Miriam always seemed to have on hand, no matter how unexpected the visit.

There is another source for my collection of tiny toys, a small box that belonged to my mother. I still have it but it's too fragile now for five-year-olds to play with. The small cardboard box is painted rich brown and lined with cotton. There is a glass top carefully glued in place so you can see inside the box without opening it. The box is securely tied with a long dark brown shoelace. I don't know where it came from or what it represented.

If I were sick in bed, or sometimes on a quiet afternoon, my mother would bring out the little treasure box. Inside are a china baby doll less than an inch high; a peach pit carved into the shape of a basket with a handle; a bright quartz stone, several tiny seashells, and a marble tombstone, an inch and a quarter high carved with a cross and inscribed "Jeff." As there were no Jeffs in my family, and my mother brought the box with her from her home in southern Georgia, I have always wondered if the tombstone might be a memorial to Confederate President Jefferson Davis. I wonder who collected the tiny things and who carved the peach pit basket and I've tried most of my life to ferret out the story of the box. Maybe there is no story. Maybe the tiny toys that fascinated me as a child were like my own collection – just small, pretty things to keep children occupied while ladies eat cherry pie or pound cake and drink lemonade.

Women and children have been visiting in much the same way for generations. My mother taught me early the strict rules of visiting. Men visited too, on Sundays after church, but when my mother and my aunts were young few women worked outside the home, and visiting was their obligation as well as their pleasure. A visit let friends and family know you cared about them and wanted to see them. And the refreshments they offered let you know your visit was welcome.

Visiting is an art easy to lose when we go out to work every day. Women who work get together for lunch, which is visiting in a minor key. Visiting requires small talk, the discussion of a new book or club news or something going on at a local church or some new store everybody must see. An accomplished visitor remembers details about friends' families and never forgets to ask if a sister is feeling better or if a husband's shoulder has mended or if a child has recovered from some illness. Visiting isn't just something you can do once a year and get it right.

With two incomes so essential in the modern American home, we seem to be reverting to the ancient tribal practice of turning the care of young children over to grandparents, an essential job they're well trained to do. A great deal is being written about what a chore it is for grandparents to have to take on child care after they've worked hard all their lives and earned the right to a perpetual vacation.

But maybe instead of a vacation that never ends, what grandparents really want is to feel needed, to know they still have a role to play in the society they live in. Strengthening the bond between grandparents and grandchildren is the most natural thing in the world and good for all concerned. Left to their own devices, grandparents might revive the art of the visit. Even teach it to a younger generation.

When Madi tired of the tiny toys I closed up the box and put it away and gave her the big toy basket with the dolls and blocks and cars and coloring books and crayons. And the rain fell gently, splashing on the leaves and branches outside and Kay and I sipped our lemonade and talked quietly and the music played softly. We made memories that afternoon, and life was good.

When Guests Leave

How poignant it is to stroll through an empty house when guests have just climbed into their cars after a happy visit. They back out of the driveway, waving goodbye as they speed away and you turn and open the door and experience an overwhelming sense of loss.

It was that way on Sunday when the last of the family started back home again. I walked through to the back of the house and found on a corner table a bright Navajo-pattern cocktail napkin where someone had rested a glass of wine on Friday. The toys and boxes, cups and dolls and blocks and trucks that grandson Jack had collected from all corners of the house lay scattered like bright beads on the rug just as Jack had dropped them.

In the living room I absently fluffed pillows and set them in place, picked up magazines and stacked them. There is nothing really to do, at first, when guests have just gone home.

I remember feeling an identical sense of loss when I was a child and the members of my mother's family would leave after a visit. They came fairly often and there was always as great a fuss and flurry in their leaving as there was in their coming, because visits in those days might last weeks or even a month, and include husband, wife, children, a maid to help with the extra work and at least one family pet.

They traveled with old-fashioned steamer trunks, these extended families. Mere travel cases couldn't have held all they needed to bring. The husband – one of my uncles – would spend a short time with us and then he had to get home, he would say, and go to work, doing whatever it was that men did. My own father left every morning to work in New York City and I had no interest in his life. The words skyscraper, office, company, city were colored a dull slate grey, while at home in a house full of the comings and goings of women and children and dogs and cats and rabbits and goldfish and songbirds, the games we played, the swings out back, the balls to bounce and the bicycles to ride – there was action and color, the stuff of Real Life.

My favorite visiting playmates were my cousin John, who was two years older than I, and my cousin Jim, who was two years younger. Boys close to my age were exciting companions for a little girl with two older sisters. In the wintertime, John and I liked to find dangerous places to sled. There was a sloping hill in our town, a street, in fact, several blocks long, closed to traffic so children could sled till we were too tired to drag back up the snowy slope and we would start for home with frozen toes, dragging our sleds and stumping along on feet that felt like blocks of wood unattached to our bodies. In the warm house, dripping snowsuits draped over drying rods, we would sit on the side of the bathtub with our feet in cold water to reduce the pain of thawing.

I idolized John, who taught me how to pour lead soldiers to make my own army, and possessed a larger library than my own. But when Jim was around I had the exciting sense that I was skirting dangerously close to infringing parental law. Jim and I cut saplings in the woods to build a fort, collected fireflies in Mason jars on summer evenings, raced ferociously along the sand on wide white Carolina beaches in a desperate contest to find the most sand dollars. On a visit to Jim's house one time he taught me how to shoot a .22 rifle, something I can safely say I would never have learned at home. Jim and I fell into creeks, wrecked bikes and I once hit a baseball that struck the side of the house perilously close to a dining room window. We jumped from the garage roof holding umbrellas to see if we could fly. "Don't be prissy," Jim would say in his languid South Carolina drawl. "I dare you." And of course I had to take the dare.

After a visit, summer or winter, the Railway Express truck would call at the house and the belts around the trunks would be cinched tighter and the trunks would be carried away to ride in the boxcars of trains heading south. My father would leave his work to drive the departing family to the railway terminal at Newark to catch the crack streamliner on the Seaboard Line. The car would back out of the driveway and everyone would wave and we would call out, "Telephone when you get home so we'll know you're all right."

Then we would close the front door and go back inside the house and my mother would say it might be a good time for a little nap and I would wander through rooms echoing with emptiness, teary eyed from lonesomeness and loss. There on the card table was the Monopoly game, unfinished; there on the floor the soldiers drawn up in battle order, abandoned before the winner was brevetted to higher rank. There was nothing a child could do except pick up a book and lose herself in stories of other people in other places.

Walking through our house this Sunday I marvel that the feeling of intense loss when loved guests depart hasn't changed in a lifetime. Candles burnt low on the dining room table had lighted long conversations after food. There was the jar of baby food a grandson had only partly finished, the Scrabble game on the hearth where Jim and Chris had left it, Jeni's scrapbooks full of family pictures she had brought to share, and everywhere the faint echo of talk and laughter, like the fragrance of yesterday's flowers lingering in airy, empty rooms.

There was little that a child could do to ease the loss when beloved guests departed. And though I feel the loss today as I felt it as a child, I am not a child anymore and the weekend was busy and active and the nights were full and late. I catch myself weighing the benefits of a little nap. How like our mothers we all become, I think, finding the irony delicious.

LONG AUTUMN THOUGHTS

The long-awaited arrival of a new hot tub from its factory in Georgia washed our thoughts clean of drought, war, politics and other perils of modern life. The tub arrived on a September afternoon, delivered by a big truck with an automatic tailgate. The trucker pulled into our neighbor's driveway and backed close to the althea hedge at the property line and the tailgate whined down and then up and there was our hot tub, swathed like a very large baby nestled in our neighbor's gravel.

At the althea hedge the neighbor's driveway is level with the terrace at the back of our house. We have a long-standing deal to route heavy deliveries that way. Keeps us from having to haul hot tubs down hazardous steep grades.

I pick up the telephone and call next door. "Just thought I'd let you know there's a hot tub in your driveway," I say. "We'll have it out of there as soon as the wrecking crew arrives."

"Looks like a good one," our neighbor says. "No hurry."

At 6 p.m. a quintet of husky family males picks up the hot tub and begins a staggering progress through the althea bushes, around the pear tree, across the terrace, up the steps and over the downstairs deck. It's as slow as a funeral procession and not without incident.

"Don't worry," grandson Chris tells me. "It's only a small dent, and it's on the side next to the wall."

Like kids at Christmas we have our bathing suits on and towels over our arms and are headed downstairs just about the time dawn breaks the next morning. Crunching through an overnight shower of leaves on the deck, we feel the morning chill on bare skin and lower ourselves into hot water. "Ahh," we say, letting the jets pummel us and watching the sun light up our world.

Signs of autumn are everywhere, in fallen leaves crisp as cornflakes, in slanting morning light and cooler days. One morning last week I walked out on the porch and found the decking cold against my bare feet and the temperature standing at 59 degrees. "Oh no!" I thought, not ready yet to downshift to a new season.

In summer we troll the lake, work on the decks and in the garden, sweep porches and sidewalks, deadhead blooms, host friends and family, pull weeds, clip foliage, then settle into a deck chair and pick up a glass of iced tea in one hand and a book in the other. Now suddenly it's fall and the big urns full of summer flowers have taken on new life, their bloom thicker, their colors brighter these cool autumn days after the rain.

Inside, it's a different story. I look around the house and catch signs of summer neglect. "What a mess!" I mutter, getting out my car keys for a tomato run to Hartsburg. Jo Hackman says her farm market tomatoes are like my summer flowers, never better than in September when you know a killing frost could be only weeks away. With my tomatoes I buy a handful of decorative gourds and bring them home and arrange them in a big basket with autumn leaves and set the basket in front of the fireplace. First you arrange the flowers. Then you clean the house.

In a manner of speaking I've been arranging the flowers all week, changing the cushions on the porch furniture, pulling a colorful old quilt out of storage to toss over the back of a chair on the porch. I bought a new watercolor, "By the Stream," and a pastel named "Old Acorn" at the historical society's art auction. They need framing and I start going round the color wheel and making lists of change-of-season chores.

It's time to take my lists to town. Only Wal-Mart could turn warehouses into retail sales clubs with membership fees, I think, wheeling a Sam's Club cart through aisles stacked high with boxes. This is not a buying trip, just your basic scoping stop and I have time to drift, visiting sections I rarely see – small appliances, electronics, tools, furniture.

In the middle of office furniture I run into old friend Susie Nichols. I'm checking out a new chair for my home office and she's looking for a standing-height desk for her computer. It's just after I turn a corner stacked high with recliners that I glance across a thoroughfare aisle and see it, a display of prancing reindeer and a swift little sleigh outlined in white lights, and I say "Ahh," under my breath.

Where did that "Ahh" come from? Like everybody else I mutter about stores putting out Christmas merchandise before we've carved our jack-o-lanterns (give us a break). But the prancing reindeer flashed before my wondering eyes before I had time to pull on my indignation, and I said "Ahh" and thought "Christmas!" and happiness flowed in uninvited.

That "Ahh" came from sitting in the hot tub that morning thinking about cold winter nights when the tub is a haven in a world of falling snow. Where there is snow, can Christmas be far behind? Our tub is under roof so the snow falls all around and you look out at it and feel as if you're defying the elements, as if you're thumbing your nose at the weather and saying, "So go ahead and snow. Who cares?"

Then I thought about the resort club in Burlington, Wisconsin just down the road from the big white house we lived in long ago. The swim pavilion was attached to the resort's main building, just a pool in a big room with a lofty glass ceiling and walls. Swimming there in Wisconsin's long cold winters, with steam rising inside and new snow falling on old snow outside, was the heart of joy. The pool was never crowded. Hardy local folk were out snowmobiling and ice fishing and racing cars on the frozen lake and they couldn't fathom why puny foreigners like us wanted to dress up in bathing suits and go swimming in the middle of winter.

Stepping out of the hot tub these cool autumn mornings is a reminder that winter may be a long way off but it's not too early to start closing a few windows and doors. You know summer is over when you light candles in the evening and the kitchen smells of hearty soups and sweet cinnamon apples baking.

Early fall is an optimum time to break in a new hot tub, a place to dream about good old fall and winter days and plan your Christmases, present and future. The thoughts that take root when you're afloat in a hot tub can be long thoughts, likely to lead almost anywhere. To an "Ahh" of surprise and pleasure, for instance, turning a corner at Sam's Club, of all places, on a Saturday afternoon in September.

Through Revolving Doors

We go back a long way together, Chris and Dick and I. When Chris was born I moved to his house for a week and held my first grandchild and rocked him in the small hours of the night so his mother could get some sleep. Later, when his parents' marriage ended, as marriages sometimes do, Chris and his mother came to live with us in the big house south of Centralia. He was a sturdy three year old with a practical turn of mind. We constructed a sandpit behind the treeline in the big pasture and he built roads there and mountains and stuck branches in the ground to make trees. He had an old wooden chest to pack his trucks in to keep them out of the rain.

Chris was commissioned last Friday night in the U. S. Army, Second Lieutenant Bradley, chemical weapons officer, 3rd Armored Cavalry. His family walked round and round him, examining every detail of the immaculate uniform. The gold bars on his shoulders, pinned there by his mother and father. The ribbons from his training and the National Guard, the insignia for National Guard service in Germany.

When he was three or four years old his grandfather brought him toys from Germany. In those days he loved to sit on the kitchen counter and cook with his mother, or play on the long rope swing in the backyard, or ride shotgun on the big power mower while granddad drove, or soothe my fear of spiders and snakes. His mother worked the night shift at University Hospital so we put Chris to bed, chasing the monsters out of his closet before the final poems and prayers, maybe a little backrub and a quiet song.

At Fairview Elementary School Chris studied Spanish; at Hickman High School, three years of Latin. He fought the good fight on the wrestling team and played football there and later at Westminster College. His family swelled with pride when as class president he gave the address at the Hearnes Center for his high school graduation.

Jane Duncan Flink

Chris grew up with the blessings of an even disposition, a tendency to be task-oriented, an inquiring mind and an extended loving family. He wasn't the sort of child who minded if his grandmother hugged him in public. As a teenager he traveled in the backseat on a cross-country trip by car to my family's home in New Jersey. Climbing in every morning he would ask, "What can we talk about today?" and it might be George Washington, or the mystery of Stonehenge or what stars are for.

He's traveling cross-country again this week, on Army time this time, to a Special Forces camp in Washington State, then to Fort Benning with an Air Force detachment, and finally to Fort Leonard Wood to study chemical warfare.

Little boys are fragile creatures, far more fragile than little girls. Little girls don't change much when they grow into big girls. They are still smart and pretty and capable. But sweet boy babies sooner or later must learn to be men, very different creatures indeed, and a grandmother can only blend rejoicing with mourning, searching the face of the Distinguished Cadet for a trace of the sweet child she misses so much, the child that is gone forever.

We have always been close, Chris and Dick and I, through school and college and on to graduate school and the Army. Study Chinese, I told him one day as we sat talking about life under the shade of a big tree in our backyard. He enrolled in Chinese that year and later studied Arabic, trying unsuccessfully to teach us the alphabet. He calls me on the phone from grad school. "I need to know more about the Battle of Saratoga and I've done the books so I'm calling my old history pal. What can you tell me?"

Friday night, May 19: the commissioning is an ending and a beginning. When the ceremony is over we say goodbye, achingly aware that there won't be any more weekend drop-ins at dinner time, Chris bringing friends and fellow students from Nigeria or the Ukraine, a chef from New York City, a poet from the hills of Arkansas. No more fishing trips with his granddad, no more long talks over a glass of Shiraz about his research into the structure of the military, my latest literary puzzle or what it means to think in Arabic.

Committed now to work that is essential, work that can be dangerous, Chris closes a door that framed a life of striving and ease, labor and love. In front of him another door opens on a future that is peculiarly his own. Doors revolve in everybody's life, doors that close and doors that open, each warning that this is a time for reflection. Street lights beam down on Springfield, inviting us to linger on a threshold bathed in light, the reflection of a lifetime of shining moments. But Chris can find those places in memory, and this day is done. He snaps to attention, tosses a final salute to his uncle, the Colonel, and turns and walks away. He's in the Army now.

Friendships Can Last A Lifetime

When we met, nothing indicated we'd be lifelong friends. Dick's job had taken our family from New York to suburban Milwaukee. He made contact there with his college classmates, Shirley and Jerry, who lived nearby. Before many weeks went by they were on their way to our house to share a meal.

That first meeting was not a success. The men picked up where they left off while Shirley and I circled each other, cool and polite. She found me way too East Coast precious. I was irritated by her Midwestern bluntness. "Is there a moment between that first meeting and the time when you *become* friends?" asks Patricia O'Brien in the book she co-authored with Ellen Goodman, "I Know Just What You Mean." The book is about the enduring friendship between O'Brien, journalist and novelist, and Goodman, newspaper columnist and author.

In the beginning, Shirley and I, thrown together by our husbands' attachment, focused on bringing our same-age children together. We shared a lifestyle, both of us stay-at-home moms in our 20s with corporate executive husbands who traveled a lot. It was the 1950s and we each had a new ranch house and a big green lawn. There was one car per family and the men took it to work. In that daytime world, women counted on each other for everything from comfort during postpartum depression to borrowing a box of baby cereal or hitching a ride to town from anybody who had the family car for the day. Starved for adult conversation, Shirley and I began talking on the phone, tentatively exploring our shared interest in the arts, books and politics. We found we enjoyed oddball topics like what it means to have a dolichocephalic head shape and tagging our kids with tendencies to be endomorph, mesomorph or ectomorph.

When a new church went up in the neighborhood, we joined the choir. She sang alto and I sang soprano. Like the blend of our voices, our growing friendship was based on the way we complemented each other. We're the same height but not the same size. Shirley is lean and blonde, reflecting her Danish ancestry. My Scots heritage gave me long legs and a sturdy body. Her no-nonsense ways reflect her North Dakota roots. My deep South background can lead me to fix my eyes on the stars and stub my toe on a rock.

All of her life, Shirley fought to gain weight. From the time my first baby was born, I fought to keep it off. I am heated, impulsive, assertive, I like to get things done. Shirley is cool, analytical and reserved. I am a writer. She is an artist. As the children grew, I took my talent to the workplace. She took hers into juried art shows and active membership in Mensa.

Through it all, we talked. Goodman writes, "A woman friend calls another and says, 'I have to talk.' And what they both know is, if she doesn't, the big problem or the small dilemma will stick in her throat like a fishbone. At the heart of the connection is the sentence that became the book title – a sentence friends say to each other: 'I know just what you mean.'"

Shirley and I have both said, "That time, you saved my life." Her family is three girls and one boy. Mine is three girls and two boys. "Let me take her for a few days," one of us would say when the other was struggling with a rebellious child. "Let's see if we can't get to the bottom of this behavior." The obstreperous child would spend a few days under new management and return home, tension eased. When I was bedridden with a difficult pregnancy, Shirley, juggling her own family, installed me in her guestroom for a weekend. She and the children took turns bringing me magazines and books, meals on trays, conversation, and stern admonitions to keep my feet elevated at all times.

Inevitably, in time our husband's jobs took us in different directions. We were neighbors in Wisconsin and again in St. Louis before their family left for four years in Scotland and our daily telephone calls became weekly letters thick with pages in envelopes tricked out with a kaleidoscope of stamps. Home again, they settled near the Cape in Florida and I spent a week with them one winter because my friend needed a friend and telephone calls weren't enough.

Shared experience and laughter deepen the friendships I share with a remarkable group of women in my Boone County home. Keeping a friend sometimes means knowing when to back off, knowing what not to say, never being afraid to say you're sorry. Years ago I said something thoughtless to Linda, a friend who lived next door. I couldn't think of a better remedy, so the next day I carried a bouquet of flowers to her house, wondering what I would say when I got there. When she opened the door I held out the flowers and said, "I'm sorry. It was my fault." Linda cocked her head, grinned at me and took the flowers. "Never mind," she said. "An old Chinese proverb says we allow our friends three faults." And our friendship went on.

Goodman and O'Brien write, "...the solid thing friends get out of a long-term friendship is truly knowing someone and being known. There are few enough people in life who can freely reveal themselves to each other, who keep each other's interests at heart. When you find it, cherish it ..."

And that can mean going the extra mile – literally. Our family flew to Santa Fe for Shirley and Jerry's fiftieth wedding anniversary. They were here for Dick's eightieth birthday party. These days, e-mails fly back and forth almost every day with talk of my writing projects, her new technique in colored pencil drawing, books, their new condo in Mesa, Arizona, children and grandchildren, politics, religion, travel, philosophy, the revolution that will be sparked by the introduction of the nitrogen-powered automobile and the phrase that has opened a thousand dialogues between us, "Have you ever considered . . ?"

A friend talks. Better still, a friend listens. Friendship is precious because it isn't licensed or required. There are no vows, no documents, no bans, no laws. There are no guidelines, no legalities to prevent a friendship from dissolving on any day at any time. No tests to pass to keep it intact save those of abiding love and understanding. Friendship thrives on due diligence, appreciation and thoughtfulness and when these are present, freely given and received, a friendship, more flexible than a family tie, can last a lifetime.

An Independent Fourth Of July

In retirement, you betray yourself. "Never give up," said Winston Churchill. "Never, never, never." But the unstructured life is seductive. In the early stages, you hate it. As time goes by you teach yourself to tolerate it. Inevitably, the morning comes when you take a look at the free and uncluttered day ahead of you and smile smugly. "Oh, baby," you breathe. "You've got it made."

On the Fourth of July in years past we couldn't wait to get to Kansas City for Jim and Jamie's annual party. We arrived to find the baked beans bubbling, the potato salad chilling, the bratwurst and Italian sausage thawing, beer and soft drinks flowing, and a dozen or so guests blowing up balloons for what looked like a kindergarten class from a local school. There were little kids everywhere, any one of them capable of making more noise than a Black Cat rocket.

One year, a mother made red white and blue star-spangled crowns for the kids to wear as they ran screaming through the house. "It's good to see you," I yelled at one of Jim's friends. "You too!" the friend screamed back. By 9 p.m., parents gathered up kids and the house emptied out as everybody trooped to a vantage point on Riss Lake where fireworks ring the horizon. The party wound up with a red, white and blue cake and we lit the candles and everybody sang Happy Birthday to Uncle Sam.

The party, by any standard, was a huge success but when we were invited to come again this year, we said, "Gosh, thanks so much, but we just can't make it." The thanks are sincere – it's a gift to be wanted. But this July Fourth, we opted to let the days slide by, taking things as they come. This July Fourth would be our personal holiday.

It had occurred to us a few years ago that we talk about American independence and have thrown our share of long, hot, noisy July Fourth parties. But most of our knowledge of the revolution came from fourth grade textbooks. So we went on a reading binge, aware immediately that history today has more complexities than a massacre on Boston Commons and a terrible winter at Valley Forge. Historians and biographers used to fight for rare access to the Founding Families' letters, and page through acres of moldy card files. Computer technology has changed all that, and books, films and the Internet are crammed with new information about the stubborn visionaries who gave the world a new form of governance to sample.

On Sunday night, we planned a quiet evening at home with time out to welcome fireworks at Lake Champetra. Dick put the ribs on the grill, and we switched the remote to the History Channel to watch the Revolutionary War unfold. The focus was on George Washington's army and the genius of its commander. Washington learned early that he didn't have to win the war, he had only to not lose it. It wasn't about defending territory. His army personified the revolution, and we tasted victory in part because he concentrated on preserving, supplying and maintaining a fighting force.

The TV story began after the citizens of North Carolina rose up against their royal governor, after Sam Adams named a Liberty Tree in Boston.

We watched British soldiers march on Breed's Hill and followed Ben Franklin to France where it wasn't till after our victory at Saratoga that he could persuade the French to ally with the colonists. With France and America pitted against Britain, our revolution became a transatlantic war fought from the islands of the Caribbean to the borders of Canada.

When the History Channel ended its story of the revolution and the fireworks began popping over the lake, we stepped out into the hot, black night to hear the booms and catch the dazzle above the trees. Nick the dog barked his objection at the stars, and Murphy the cat slid into the house and under a chair. At Riss Lake, we thought, hosts and guests would be gathering up sleepy children and aiming for the blessings of quiet bedrooms.

Our own cool quarters beckoned but we lingered longer, unwilling to detach from the strength of the Great Ones. We had spent an evening with Washington, Jefferson, Adams, Franklin, Madison, Paine, Henry, Greene, Morgan, Gage and a luminous supporting cast. In such company by any standard, our Fourth of July party was a success. We lingered lazily, leaning against deck railings in the still night, waiting for the tree frogs to recover from the rockets' red glare and pick up the melody of their homely evening songs

THE ELEPHANT YOU NEVER FORGET

I wanted an elephant. I didn't know I wanted an elephant. What I wanted was a table to go between two new chairs on the upstairs deck. On Saturday morning I cleared away all the old furniture, gave the deck a good cleaning, and stood back to set the design elements in my mind. The deck never looks the same two summers in a row. This year, it will match the screen porch you walk through on your way to the deck, rich with tropical accents.

All I had to work with were a few large tubs of flowers, a giant banana tree, half a dozen green plants and the two new deck chairs that are marvels of construction. They would be right at home on a Hawaiian lanai. They recline, taking up a lot of space, or fold up very small. They have the sort of fabric that the rain drains through and they dry fast. They have footrests and little awnings to keep the sun off your face. They look like nothing so much as a pair of giant praying mantises.

It was a perfect work day, warm with late April sun and I had just finished planting two big tubs with flowers from the Ashland Garden Club sale when Dick wandered around to the deck to try out the new chairs. I leaned on the railing and told him that we needed a table to go between the chairs, a table for a glass of tea and a book and maybe some sunglasses and having fractured my budget buying the chairs, I was trying to think of how to come by a table at low or no cost.

"There's this project I saw on HGTV," I said, ignoring Dick's lowered eyebrows. He is very, very tired of HGTV. A designer on one of the shows made a table by taking two good-sized terra cotta pots and turning one of them upside down. Then she glued the bases of the two pots together. She filled the top pot halfway with sand and the rest of the way with colorful pebbles. After that, all you have to do is run to the store and buy a round glass tabletop and set it on the rim of the top pot and you can see the pebbles through the glass. On HGTV it looked like one snazzy table.

Dick thought about it, his eyes on a pod of giant carp scarfing up grass clippings and leaves in the lake water down in our cove. He thought some more, watching the hummingbirds fighting over the red flowers in the big pots. "If you want a table that doesn't cost anything, don't forget the elephants," he said.

A light bulb went off in my head. I had completely forgotten that two years ago Dick found a pair of plaster elephant tables at a garage sale and brought them home and I cheered, because I have always loved elephants (having been exposed at an early age to Tarzan movies). But those elephants need a major paint job, so they've been pushed farther and farther back into a corner of our disgraceful garage, becoming the sort of stored treasure you're going to get to one of these days.

I perked up at mention of the elephants, and Dick said carelessly, "Or I can get you the elephant I have in my trunk." For a minute I thought I'd had too much sun. Elephant? Trunk? "In the trunk of my car," he explained. You have an elephant in the trunk of your car? Yep, he said, and if I wanted to see it, he'd go get it.

He found this elephant at another garage sale, of course, but this is not your ordinary elephant. This elephant has a bronze finish with touches of green; a caparisoned elephant with jewels on his forehead, bearing a tray on his back which might be the foundation for a howdah with silk curtains where a princess of India would ride, like the pictures in my grandmother's encyclopedia. A perfect elephant for a tropical deck in the summertime. No painting required.

I ran to the store for pebbles for the tray and the round glass for the top and finished up the deck and we spent Sunday afternoon lolling in the new chairs while Dick read Tom Clancy and I read *The New Yorker*. We set our glasses of iced tea on the glass top of the elephant table and watched a wren build a nest in a flowerpot and listened to the lake water lapping the shores of the cove and even at dinner time, we didn't want to go inside.

There's a wonderful little poem in one of A. A. Milne's Christopher Robin books that begins, "Jonathan Joe had a mouth like an O and a wheelbarrow full of surprises…." The poem lists the things a child might crave, and Jonathan Joe has all of them in his wheelbarrow.

In the 50-plus years we've been married, more than once I've thought maybe Jonathan Joe lives with me under an assumed name. Early on we had one car and Dick drove it to work. Eventually I bought a second-hand small sedan that ran when it felt like it. One year on my birthday Dick invited me out to dinner and we dressed up and he asked me if I would mind if we stopped by the car dealership on the way, because he needed to talk to Fred about something. We walked into the showroom and Fred came out with a big grin and Dick waved his hand and told me, "Pick out whatever you want." When I got over the shock, I owned a brand new yellow convertible with black leather seats and four on the floor and the biggest engine the company made.

That was the holymoly of all surprises, the one you never forget, but the surprises never quit coming. Need new barstools? Well, it just happens that I have…or here, I think this frame will fit that picture…or, that trowel you're working with isn't sturdy enough, try this one…or you said you couldn't find ferns, come tell me what you think of these.

For obvious reasons, the car steals the show in this story. But the elephant is closing fast. Who could ever forget that on an ordinary Saturday afternoon when my need for a table was strong enough that I was ready to settle for two flowerpots glued together, somehow we got around to elephants and my true love said to me, "You want an elephant? I've got one in the trunk of my car." If you drop by our house we'll be glad to show you our elephant. But if your imagination carried you far afield when I mentioned the howdah with the silk curtains and the princess of India, I'm afraid you're on your own.

The Survey Says…

You get surveys. You get them in the mail, people call you on the telephone. Surveys show up in magazines and newspapers and in the mail box on your computer desktop. On days when you can say, "What the hey, I've got time," maybe you play along, not taking it seriously. Surveys are like fortune cookies – you do the drill for the fun of it. Or you drop the survey into the nearest round file, or tell the caller no thanks and hang up the phone.

Late last year a serious survey popped up on my computer screen. It took me a minute to tell what it was. It came from Cornell University, from a close friend's daughter. Barbara is an instructor in psychology there and like a true child of the Ya Ya Sisterhood, when she took on a project about women who live long lives, she sent the survey to her mother and to me.

I like this survey right away. I like it a lot. It consists of a single question: "What have you learned from your life?" and there's a handy little box to write in with a neat vertical line blinking invitingly as if to say, "Come on – you can tell *me*."

What a gift for a writer! When I compose newspaper columns, I know my readers will scan the first few lines and if the topic interests them they'll keep on reading. If not, they'll turn to the sports page or the movie review.

It's not like that with this survey. This one goes to a captive audience – a group of Ph.D.s breathless to know what I've learned from living, a sobering thought. You do learn things if you live for a long time, but it's hard to find anybody who wants to hear about it. What tone should I take in my reply? I want the authors of the survey to read what I write and find it useful. No small humorous asides – psychologists have an inherent fear that people are laughing at them. No irony. These are dedicated, serious, scientific people. They don't find pleasure in irony.

Keep it short, I tell myself. There will be thousands of these things crossing the researchers' desks. Have mercy on them.

The knottiest problem is the question itself. A long life is a long time and we learn something new every day of our lives. In math, I learned that pi equals 3.1416. History teaches me that it's senseless to worry about the world because humankind repeats the same mistakes endlessly.

When I was young, I studied the French language and was taught when the temperature dips, the French say, "Il fait froid," or "It makes cold." I learned to use a computer when I was 45 years old. I have almost always known that it's wise to weigh expert testimony, because experts don't always agree. I sometimes had trouble with my teachers in school because they insisted on just one answer to a question, when I could see at least three.

In Latin I was taught, "Gallia est omni divisa in partes tres." My father was taught "Omnia Gallia in partes tres divisa est" and he scolded my Latin teacher while I stared fixedly at the floor. Somehow I feel that none of this is the sort of thing the psychologists want to hear.

"What have you learned from your life?" How do you choose from so much richness? The little vertical bar blinks patiently but insistently. It is time to rein in my random thoughts and begin to write:

- Be kind to people. Most of them deserve it.

- Give your family and friends your undying loyalty.

- Remain flexible. Your life won't turn out the way you thought it would.

- Quit complaining. You have to play the hand that's dealt you.

- Only you can choose to be happy or unhappy. Choose to be happy. A survivor of a Nazi death camp in the 1940s said being there taught him that his enemies could destroy his family, strip him of his wealth; they could beat him, starve him, work him to death. The only thing they could not control was his attitude.

- Learn all you can about everything you can. Life is beautiful. Cozy up to it and share its confidences.

- You are made up of the physical, the emotional, the intellectual and the spiritual. If one of these is out of order, give it your time and attention until your life is back in balance.

- Remember the lessons your mother and father taught you. Use them as your guiding stars. In their minds they weren't only raising a child, they were creating the future.

- Pray often. God has things to tell you.

As I read over what I wrote, I think a little editing would improve it. But to edit is to introduce second thoughts. Only that first stream of consciousness is entirely uncorrupted. I think about the psychologists who will receive my words along with the thousands of words from people all over the country, and I wish I could read over their shoulders. I want to know what other people have learned from living. But that isn't the way this game is played. My job is done.

I read what I have written one last time and think, "Is that all there is, in such a long life?" No, of course there is more, even things as weighty as these. But here are listed the things I couldn't do without, hard to learn, some of them,, and harder to keep. They spring to mind because they made a difference and in all of it, I am content. I lean forward, position the cursor, and click "Send."

Happily Ever After

Once upon a time a boy met a girl and it was love at first sight. He loved her sweetness, her softness, her tiny waist and the way her eyes flashed with mischief or startled, doe-like. And she loved his profile in reverie, his slow smile, his warm hands and the feeling he gave her that she was safe as long as he was there.

One thing led to another and in time they committed to love each other forever and they were married and played house together and began their life doing everything as a pair, which took some getting used to.

Time passed and the perfect babies came and her tiny waist expanded and her eyes looked tired and had dark circles under them. And his reveries turned to bringing papers home to work on and he smiled his slow smile less often and when he was working late sometimes she felt alone and abandoned.

They began doing things as a family because they put the children first and those were good times. They moved to a bigger house and she and the children were busy and they laughed a lot and he went about his business and they honored their commitment because of the children but they hardly ever did anything together, just the two of them, anymore.

In time the perfect babies turned into sharp-tongued teenagers, impatient with their parents, and one by one they went off to educate themselves and find loves of their own. And she got a new job making her own money and bought new clothes and a new car and her doe-like eyes sparkled with adventure and excitement that had nothing to do with him, and he felt alone and abandoned.

There came an evening when they looked across the room at each other in their big, quiet house and smiled politely and she thought, "I can't remember why I married him," and he thought, "I don't even know this woman anymore."

Now they had time to travel together so they went to romantic places but they didn't feel very romantic and sometimes silently they thought it might be more fun to be with someone else. But that wasn't their way and they vowed instead to be kind to each other and if they were less committed to their love, they were still committed to their commitment and life was good. Enough.

The years went by, their passing hardly noticed, and the days came when they toasted their children at their weddings and they realized they had no advice to offer them except to live responsibly, honor their commitment and try to keep their love alive.

Time passed and one day they were moving a piece of furniture to make room for a grandchild to visit and they jostled each other and she looked at him with mischief in her eyes and gave him a little push on purpose, and he smiled his slow smile and wrapped his arms around her and hugged her hard and it reminded them both of the good old days. And pretty soon when they came into the house they would call to each other as they used to do, and they did everything as a pair again, comfortably, and sometimes his warm hand held hers when they walked together down the street.

One night when dinner was over and there were no children on the telephone and no meetings to go to and nobody was having a party and he was reading his book and she was reading hers, something in the book made her think back over the years they had shared.

They had carried the weight of the world on their shoulders for a long time and now they had put that burden down by the side of the road. Sometimes they missed the familiar weight of it but they had raised a handful of the next generation to pass that way and pick it up and when the time was right, pass it on.

She thought about their early love and the times when they were intense about their jobs and their children and the days when they hardly knew each other and through it all, how good it was and now this day, she thought, with a little shiver of recognition, how good it is. And he looked up and smiled his slow smile and they both knew that their story was turning out exactly as they wanted it to. There really are happy endings, she thought, surprised, because here they were together, living happily ever after.

– End –

About The Author

Jane Flink's column, "Home Again," is published weekly in the *Boone County Journal* newspaper in Ashland, Missouri. She and her husband Dick owned and published the *Journal* from 1986 until they sold the newspaper and retired in 2001.

She was born in Atlanta, Georgia and raised in Ridgewood, New Jersey, a suburb of New York City. She attended Carleton College in Northfield, Minnesota and has lived in several major cities and two small Midwestern towns. Over the last 30 years, Flink has been an award-winning reporter, photographer, editor and publisher, and is nationally recognized as a community journalist. She was president of Missouri Press Women and named that organization's Woman of the Year; She served on the board of the National Federation of Press Women and is the recipient of its National Achievement Award. She was a member of the legislative committee of the Missouri Press Association.

Flink was associate editor of *Missouri Ruralist* magazine and has written for *Lake Lifestyles* and *MacLean's* magazines, and several newspapers. She is an editorial consultant for Greenways Incorporated in Durham, North Carolina.

The Flinks edited and published the book, *Time and the River: The Great Flood of 1993*. From 1985 to 1990, she was director of the Winston Churchill Memorial and Library at Westminster College, Fulton, Missouri.

Dick and Jane are parents of five adult children. They live among the wooded bluffs of the Missouri River valley on a private lake in rural Hartsburg, Missouri.

Printed in the United States
81779LV00002B/433-639